REINVENTING THEOLOGY

AS THE PEOPLE'S WORK

by
Ian M. Fraser

formerly Dean & Head of the Dept. of Mission
Selly Oak Colleges

Illustrations by Ray Price

First Published 1980
3rd Revised Edition 1988

Other Titles by Ian Fraser include:

My Faith and My Job
Faith Comes Alive
Bible, Congregation and Community
Sex As Gift
The Fire Runs
Lets Get Moving
Live With Style
People Journeying
Wind And Fire

And Hymns in many hymn books

Printed in Great Britain by
Antony Rowe Ltd, Chippenham, Wiltshire

The Wild Goose is a Celtic symbol of the Holy Spirit
It serves as the logo of Iona Community Publications

WILD GOOSE PUBLICATIONS
The Publishing Division of The Iona Community
Pearce Institute, 840 Govan Road, GLASGOW G51 3UT
☎ (041) 445 4561

CONTENTS

3

PROLOGUE

Those who saw this manuscript in draft form were appalled or cheered by it. There was not much reaction in between.

I devalue the professional theologian? "That is what I thought at first" said Bishop Kalilombe. "But as I read on I realised that your concern is to find a much more relevant place for the theological specialist — at the heart of the life of God's people".

I make too much of developments in Selly Oak? I speak of what I am in touch with, that's all. I have no desire to play down the work of other enterprises — such as, e.g., the pioneering work of the Urban Theology Unit in Sheffield. I find very few places as concerned as Selly Oak to relate theology to living situations.

Why "reinventing"? Because theology is already there among the people, waiting to be found; at the same time there is new work to be done. In Latin the word means both 'to find' and 'to contrive'.

"It reads more like a Manifesto than a dissertation"? It was meant to.

In the end what can one do but launch the ship one has built with conviction, and see if it sails!

Frankly Dean
I am in favour of a
closed shop policy
in theology.

5

FOREWORD

Ian M. Fraser wrote *Reinventing Theology as the People's Work* in 1980 with the 1981 conference *A Theology for Britain in the 80's* and the *European Woudshoten Conference* in mind. But as it happens often in the ecumenical family, because something is relevant to one context, it becomes relevant also to other contexts and soon begins to raise some pertinent questions to all contexts. This book has helped to raise interest in people's theology outside Europe.

The Programme on Theological Education of the World Council of Churches has picked up 'Theology by the People', as one of its chief concerns in the post-Vancouver period. The concept is a sequel to its earlier and ongoing emphasis on 'Ministry by the People'. The underlying conviction is that just as ministry belongs to the whole people of God and not just to a part of the whole – the ordained clergy, so the task of theologising belongs to the whole people of God and not to a part of the whole – the professional theologian. For doing theology goes hand in hand with Christian living and reflecting on faith accompanies Christian discipleship. New forms of discipleship create new forms of theology, as new forms of theology inspire new ways of living.

An international consultation in Mexico in April 1985 explored what the theme means, what would be the processes, participants and perspectives when theology becomes people's enterprise, and the implications of all these to programmes of ministerial formation of the churches. Part of the exploration was to seek new ways of doing theology in community, and to discover new roles for academic theologians and professional clergy in that process. Some of the fruits of the consultation are now available in the WCC publication *Theology By The People*. The attempt being made is to restore people as doers of theology and searchers of the scriptures, so that they can be faithful and obedient amidst the challenges in today's world.

Reinventing Theology raises some critical questions about the present style of doing theology in Europe, and by implication, in other places where such models are preserved and pursued. The author suggests that the academic theologians will rediscover their role as enablers right at the centre of the believing community if they would choose to become part of the common life, worship and struggles of that community. He also challenges all Christians not to sell away their birthright of doing theology, but take this business seriously as a significant part of their discipleship.

Our hope is that this will make a modest contribution to the churches' task of reinventing theology as people's work.

Samuel Amirtham

Director, Programme on Theological
Education of the World Council of Churches.

1985

Note: When, as a member of the Iona Community, Ian entered industry in 1942 as the first of what became a worker-priest/pastor movement, he was challenged to justify such action on top of an MA and BD with distinction in Systematic Theology. He said, at that time, that his action did not mean the abandonment of ministry but a search for authentic ministry, nor the abandonment of theology but a search for a more relevant theology. The concern of this book has accordingly been a life-long preoccupation.

Ed.

GOD AND MAN LET DOWN

Does it matter that theology has for long denied its nature and been diverted from its tasks?

The defect has not proved to be a slip of the consciousness with little harm done, but a damaging betrayal of humanity. When the subjects of theology cover no more than the immediate concerns of churchmen, the field is left clear for ruthless shaping powers, which have no interest in life running God's way but their own way, to occupy the field.

A church all tied up with salvation and damnation questions tidily separated from the reality of life – as if salvation and damnation floated above us rather than were at the heart of our struggles – duly proved to be in no condition to encourage people to recognise what was at stake at the time of the Clearances in Scotland. When people's houses were burnt over their heads and they were driven out of their lands in favour of sheep and deer, theology was being discussed over cups of tea, or brought into play to legitimise the injustice.

Its own damnation is written in the disinterest of the working classes, the irrelevance it has long held for the exploited.

Look up! In our time a new thing is happening. People are breaking free from systems of deprivation. Theology is no exception. It is being reinvented as the people's work.

NEW ERA IN THEOLOGY

The word "theology" describes the disciplined attempts of human beings to understand how the world has been and is being affected by God's prescence and activity within it; to make out what kind of God he is, and what is his agenda. Christian theology proposes Jesus Christ as the unique focus for this search.*

The conviction that the work can be tackled at all is based on the belief that God reveals his mind and will to human beings and looks to them to respond to him; that they are called to know him and are invited into partnership with him in his work – the renewal of creation and the fulfilment of human history.

---

* In references to God for 'he' also read 'she'.

8

Over much of the history of the church, theological work has been done in a way which

- has testified against its essential nature;
- has kept it out of the hands of those whose task it is;
- has allowed it to be dominated by the interests and fashions, thought-forms and assumptions of **one world region**.

In consequence, humanity has been substantially denied that resource for living which theology should provide. Church thinkers, instead of resisting have encouraged this defection. They have worked on two fundamental assumptions

a) that the proper subject-matter for theological reflection is the preoccupations of the church
   - as if theology did not, of necessity, have to take account of God's concern for the whole life of creation and the whole movement of humanity in history.
b) that the proper "reflectors" are academically trained specialists.
   - as if God had not equipped a body of people with gifts of the Spirit for discerning and expressing his will.

Thus those who should have ensured that theology, as a potent resource for living, was made available to humanity, were absorbed in churchy things; and this absorption conspired to push it to the fringes of interest and importance for humanity in general.

It has worked out that way, with honourable exceptions. Theology lies on the margins of life for most people. Accordingly –

The essential nature of theology has to be recovered, if this unhappy situation is to be changed. It must be seen as the fruit of converted minds, of bodies offered as living sacrifices in a world community which enters into partnership with God in his work.

a) Theology for living cannot be got from books. Books are an auxiliary aid to what can only be learned through doing God's will.

b) It cannot be the product of efforts simply to get thought straight. There has to be a vital pulse between life as it is lived in a great variety of circumstances, and God's revelation of himself. People in the thick of life, struggling to make sense of it in complex, difficult/hopeful situations, who search the scriptures together as a source of light, have the equipment to do theology.

9

They have to learn to do so, and be given confidence to do so.

c) Theology is not a matter for the drawing board. It is not, in the end, a matter for the simulated reality of the wind-tunnel. These have a proper, preparative function and place.

Theology is for those who fly.

Its quality must be decided, corrected, verified by those who take the risk of leaving safe ground.

– If this is true, it will be seen at once that much that has passed for theology does not add up to much more than fanciful embroidery on the far hem of reality.

I hold today to what I wrote almost forty years ago, drawing upon my experience in 1942-44 when I worked as a labourer/pastor in industry:

"The academic theologian tends to bite his nails about action on the part of individuals or groups which cannot be compassed by known theological categories, or checked in terms of prevailing theological thinking. But obedience to the living God must always surge beyond present theological containing walls. When Abraham went out, he knew not whither he went. The business of theology is not to circumscribe such obedient action. It is to feed on it."

(Theology and Action. Ian M. Fraser.
Scottish Journal of Theology Vol.2, No.4, Dec. 1949.)

But Abraham
you can't just up sticks
like this and go off
Into the unknown —
Its theologically
unsound....

THEOLOGICAL COMMUNITIES TAKE SHAPE

Theology is coming out of the hands of specialists and into the hands of people who walk in Abraham's way. That fact delights and disturbs.

In much of the world church, the membership is no longer leaving theology to 'theologians' but hammering it out at white heat in the fire of experience, tempering it as weaponry for the fights of life.

O Lord thou knowest I am a theologian so thou canst speak to me with great confidence ...

No longer is a prescribed, largely academic education looked to to fit people for the task. The deficiencies of such an education are now being more and more recognised – the withdrawal from the mainstream of life; the lack of lively contact with the language and daily experience of so many people; the too exclusive stress on book-knowledge; distance from a variously gifted and involved community in which to test and check insights. The theological training of Jesus, provided in the thick of life, which developed senses alert to the sights, sounds, smells, actions and inter actions of life in the streets, in homes and fields, on the lake; and which depended on wrestling in prayer and with the Scriptures to find the mind of the Father – is being appreciated afresh. To training in theological awareness and perceptiveness of this kind, all sorts of people may have access. They are seizing their chance.

No longer is a scholarly caste given the last word in judging what is of worth in the field of theology – how can those sort out wheat from chaff who have never ploughed a field? Scholars can have a part in the whole work. They are no longer allowed to corner the theology market.

11

Illiterates now make perceptive contributions to the church's theological understanding. Workpeople on the land and in industry, women, men and children, play their part in building up theological resources — body fat from which the church can draw nourishment for lean and strenuous days. At last theology is being done in community, by people with very diverse forms of experience. They provide an essential element which has been missing. Disciplined reflection which theology requires, must have a richness of doing and perceiving to work on. Contributions made by specialists, which have their valid place, form particular and important ingredients, not the dish. To make the dish, one needs the range of ingredients supplied by the people of God, drawn from their gifts and ministries and developing awareness; and those supplied from the perceptions of people who are not Christian but are serious in their search for truth and life. It takes a community, reflecting deeply on reality as it is experienced, to give theology substance and shape; a community in which every member's contribution is respected and relished as well as critically assessed that it might find its place in a communal perceiving of God and his ways and works.

One implication is this. Theology is characteristically a lay discipline — the word laos being used in its rounded sense, so that it includes, in modest proportion, the ordained and specialists (the problem has been keeping that proportion modest).

Is this so new?

Some years ago there was pointed out to me a street corner in Falkland, Fife, where, in centuries past, farm servants gathered in their free time to discuss theological matters. Certainly in Scotland there has been an interest in theology which was not confined to specialists. But before we make too much of this, we should ask — what did the farm servants discuss? The answer — issues which preoccupied clergy, such as predestination, election, free-will! In *Holy Willie's Prayer*, Robert Burns lampoons such theology:

> "O Thou, who in the heavens does dwell,
> Who, as it pleases best Thysel,
> Sends ane to heaven, an' ten to hell,
> A' for Thy glory,
> And no for ony gude or ill
> They've done afore Thee!"

The farm servants seemed to be free but they were domesticated, held captive within an imposed world of ideas. They had the means at their disposal for dealing with highly relevant theological themes, such as the ownership and use of land — a concern prominent in the Bible and preoccupying in Scotland in recent centuries. But they were caught in the system. A harmless agenda diverted their energies.

So what you are really saying is that if I think about theology it's heresy — if you do it's brilliant scholarship?

What is new today is ordinary Christians making and tackling their own theological agendas. The sign which marks the presence of God in the midst of his human family, is visible in our day:

"I will pour out my spirit in those days
Even upon slaves and slave girls."(*Joel 2.29*)

Theology — A Commonwealth

Just as no group within the church has a right to absorb for itself theological responsibilities which the whole church should assume, so no one part of the world church has the right to lay down the norms by which theology must now be developed and evaluated. A world community is at last tackling the task of doing world theology. Black theology, Liberation theology, Feminist theology, Exodus theology, Asian Action theology, Minjung theology, Reappropriation theology by basic Christian communities, for instance, draw upon reservoirs of believing and suffering other than those fastened upon by classical western theology. The world community of faith is now challenging perceptions about God and God's work which developed from too narrow a base. Long-accepted norms for theological work come under question.

Are we seeing the end of theological imperialism and the emergence of a commonwealth of knowledge of God? Every new form of theology, equally with old forms, is now open to critical judgement within the world community! Latin American women and Africans are challenging the over-dependence of Liberation Theology on an economic reading of history. They point to the neglect of other factors which mould life, such as racism and sexism. Here is a powerful sign that theology is breaking free of the stranglehold not only of individual specialists and professional schools, not only of traditional constraints, but of dominances new as well as old.

Theology is being hammered out in the local community. Its mettle is being tested in the world community, in which theologies of many kinds are developing and interacting.

Take it – but don't unwrap it !

THEOLOGY OF THE ROAD

Classical theology has felt the need to establish its credentials by means of books, heavily annotated with references, which offer the conclusions of research, backed up with carefully weighed evidence – and this has its own virtue. Only rarely do individual writers share, as the author of *Honest to God* did, struggles and doubts rather than conclusions and clarities. By contrast, the theology of the Christian community is a theology of the road. Its purpose is not fulfilled in the assembling of a deposit of insights which show where people have arrived; but in clues to God's purpose which help them to travel obediently. That, they believe, is what theology is for. The Exodus illustrates.

Moses sees a burning bush which is not consumed. What results from his curiosity in turning aside is not a theological reflection on the way in which God may address us through odd natural phenomena. What results is response to a calling. As the response is followed through, the nature of God as a liberating God becomes clearer – what had been conveyed to the mind is given substance in history, what was addressed to one becomes the possession of a people. God's initiative and the people's response supplies in the end a theological foundation for the whole way in which they are to order their life – for instance the place of slaves in households is to be governed by the experience of slavery in Egypt and liberation from it.

Theological perceptions may come almost at the same time as the summons to obedience. Or people may have to wait for them – win them through suffering and struggle. The fruit must not be forced or plucked unripe. But neither must it be undervalued. A theological foundation provides a basis for imaginative obedience, compass bearings for keeping that obedience continually checked and on course.

Many of the theological perceptions gained by a group will be so directly related to that group's particular situation that it may prove impossible to communicate to others – even to those similarly placed in life. Some action or event may throw light on a specific situation so that a small company of people see, with quite fresh clarity, what God is doing and asking of them – and the same action or event could be utterly without significance to others who are equally faithful, in another place or at a different time!

Yet we need one another's help across the globe. We need to

15

spread the light around a bit, learning from one another's attempts to offer imaginative obedience in living situations. There will be no point in looking for action-models to transfer. Situations are too different. What we may share are hints and clues which may instruct, prevent mistakes, offer encouragement.

It is essential to respect the development of each living cell in the body of the theological community. In many cases the theological insights gained in small cells may seem irrelevant in other cells; or may, as has been said, be so sewn into a particular situation that they cannot be cut loose from it and displayed. No pressure must be brought to bear on any such communities. But if real respect is offered, it would seem to be quite a fair thing to look for insights which do communicate more widely. From within my own knowledge, I believe the following examples have that wider communicating quality;

God's Authority / Secular Powers

Affirmation, illustration and confirmation of the authority of the scriptures and of the gospel faithfully lived is not normally expected to come from the harsh operations of the secular power. But the Holy Spirit is free to operate through any channel.

In a Latin American country which will be nameless, peasants working the land have banded together in basic Christian communities in which they analyse the oppressive situation in which they find themselves and gain resources from their faith to deal with it. Marxists scratch their heads over them — their analysis is so sharp; yet it is the Christian faith not the Communist philosophy which provides their dynamic. The book from which they draw their strength is entitled *Vivir Como Hermanos* (Live Like Brothers). It contains the exodus story, some sections of the New Testament, some exposition.

The words of the Bible spoke to them very directly. Nothing came home to them with such power. One day, from an unexpected quarter, the threat that that power carried to those in control of an oppressive society was ratified.

In the region in question, vaccine was imported from a neighbouring country to inoculate cattle against diseases. On one occasion instead of doing so it killed them. The peasants assuming, rightly or wrongly, that this was a deliberate plot on the part of outside interests to take their livelihood in stock-rearing away from them and capture the market, marched on the police station in the main town. The chief of police met them, and ordered them to disband. He was backed up by policemen with guns at the ready. The peasants still came on.

"Stop or we shoot!" said the chief.

"You may as well shoot us" said the peasants, "We may as well die that way as through hunger. Our livelihood is gone".

"Don't you know that I have the authority to preserve law and order in this area?" said the chief. "As the one who has that authority, I order you to disband".

At that point, a peasant took out of his pocket a copy of *Vivir Como Hermanos* and waved it in the air, saying "There is an authority above you and above us, and you and we must both bow to it". Then all the peasants took copies from their pockets, waved them in the air and shouted to the police chief that they lived under an authority which stood over every other authority.

The chief was nonplussed. "What is it you really want?" he asked. "If you have a real grievance I'm prepared to talk it through with you".

"Not when we have guns pointing at us" said the peasants.

So he sent his men away.

He then took a seat and invited the peasants to squat down around him and talk it out.

"No,no" they said, "not you on a seat and us on the ground, all seated, or all on the ground"

So the police chief sat on the ground and talked it out with them.

The next day a police search was undertaken throughout that whole area. Every piece of the Bible which could be found in the peasant huts was confiscated as subversive literature.

Baptised To Serve And Suffer

Contact with basic Christian communites in different parts of the world has helped me to discover the extent to which I am captive to stereotyped interpretations of scripture. I have constructed a framework of understanding which I have treated as if it were authoritative, when it is bound by my own mind-set, culture, class, etc.

The parable of the Wicked Husbandman had been labelled and pigeon-holed in my mind as a parable about the death of Jesus. Its commanding message came towards the end of the story.

It was Dr. Kim Kwan Suk, General Secretary of the National Council of Christian Churches of Korea, speaking at the Christian Conference of Asia's Assembly in Pinang who helped me to see it as a parable also of our baptism and what our baptism lets us in for.

He spoke about the pressure Christian communities were under in Korea. In such circumstances, we were invited to recognise the implications of the **first** part of the parable. "What was it like for those whose lives are given over to Jesus Christ? They saw fellow Christians going with empty hands to ask those in control for what was properly due to their Master. They saw them coming back from prison, from torture, broken and beaten. Some did not come back alive. How were they to react if the call came to them? The parable helped them to understand clearly the meaning of their baptism and its implications. As a result, even some of the most fearful were found faithful."*

Communion And Sharing

When a whole group comes to see some aspect of the faith more clearly, more often than not one person articulates the discovery. The response of the others will show whether this was something they were moving towards but had not quite been able to put into words, or whether it was a quite individual insight personal to the speaker.

Some years ago Father Ed de la Torre shared with me an experience which had illuminated the meaning of the Mass for him and for all those present.

Peasants had gathered for a Mass using rice cakes and wine. Afterwards they reflected on what they had done. What was in this business of sharing a little rice cake and a little wine among themselves? They were gripped by the reality of it, they drew life from it: and they struggled together to gain a better under-

---

* I describe Dr. Kim's contribution from notes I made at the time – I believe the substance is accurate, although the wording may have been a bit different.

18

standing of something so simple that went so deep. They felt they were being taught in a fundamental way, how to live. Words, ideas, pictures tumbled out on top of one another until one burst out:

"Why is it that we break the cakes into little bits, to share them among ourselves?" he asked; and answered "Because the eucharist is the feast of the poor. It says to us that, when there is not enough to satisfy our hunger, the little we have is given that we might share it. That does not mean that poverty is a good thing. When Jesus Christ spoke about what was in store for us, he spoke of a feast. We must be ready to share his abundance! But if we belong to him, if in this Mass we have become at one with him – we have also become at one with one another, and what we have we share, however little or however much that might be". Another peasant broke in. "You are right" he said "and there is one thing more. We will not accept the standards of those who make the gross national product the measure of everything. We will not say that the work of the strongest will count for most, so that they should be given a disproportionate amount of what food there is. That is not what we learn from Jesus. No, the weak, the young, the seemingly unimportant will get their full share with the others. The eucharist not only makes us one with Christ and with one another. It tells us how precious every human being is to God and reminds us that we must express that in the way we manage our life together".

The movement of the bodies, the murmurs of assent showed that, for that company, the two men had "articulated a very profound understanding of the Eucharist" as Father Ed put it.

The Gift Of Life

Among the basic Christian communities, industrial workers, workers on the land, domestic servants are sometimes described as "Third World in Europe". In Belgium I came across groups described as "Fourth World in Europe". They comprised migrant workers and illiterates.

I asked a member of one of the groups whether their habit was to work more from the analyses of situations they faced to the words of scripture, or to start with the words of scripture and see what light they threw upon problems which had to be coped with. She replied "Neither". I was intrigued. I wanted to learn more.

What interest Fourth World basic Christian communities are, above all, the rhythms of daily life. They look at the way that life proceeds, through each day, each week, each year and ask what is important in it. They keep their eyes open for any talks on the radio or articles in a paper or magazine which might help them to go deeper in their thinking. The group my contact belonged to had fastened on the act of eating.

First they dwelt on the sheer joy of having food and being able to eat, the sheer joy of being able to win enough food to satisfy the hunger of their families, the sheer joy of sharing food with others. What a grace these things held which belonged to the pattern of every day!

Next came worrying questions. There were people without food, yet there is enough food: something must have gone wrong with the sharing. There were people who turned their noses up at wholesome, nourishing food, people who were finicky in taking certain things and rejecting others, people who would not eat at the time when food had been prepared for them. Something had gone wrong with life where food was scorned or rejected. What kind of sins interfered with the natural act of eating together wholesome food when it was prepared?

The next move was into politics. It came in the most natural way. Near them was a prison. Some of the prisoners were on hunger-strike. What was so de-humanising about their position or their treatment that they would even turn against what was needed to sustain human life – to draw attention to their protest? Surely some fundamental assault on their being had taken place, whether that could be traced to physical violence or some other form of pressure on them. There were not many things in life that were more important than taking food! The group felt challenged to get to the bottom of the situation in that prison. They would make their own judgement on the situation, and see if there was anything that they could do.

I asked whether the group would consult the Bible. "Yes", came the reply, "but not for a long time – not until they have thought for maybe a year or more about what puzzles and delights them about the way life is being lived and the questions raised for them about its meaning and its claim upon them. They will go to the Bible only when they are clear about questions they want to address to it. Maybe after two years they will turn out some theological points which have proved to be of special importance to

20

them. Then they may try to put them down and make some judgement about whether their value is that they themselves are nourished, or whether there is something to share with other groups.

Francois Houtart, a sociologist in Louvain University, had received the fruits of the work of such a group. They felt that their discoveries could be communicated more widely. He had to tell them that, in his judgement, they had reached a point of clarity about some aspects of the faith for themselves; but had not yet been able to set that out so that others could be enlightened.

The Second Coming

With Raymond Fung, of the Hong Kong Industrial Mission, and others, 600 factory workers in that colony who had become Christians in the last four years, worked on the interpretation within their own life situation of the main doctrines of the Christian faith. Incarnation, crucifixion, resurrection, justification – these could be made recognisable realities, full of meaning in the Hong Kong industrial context. It was exciting to find old doctrines come alive within that very special context.

But one doctrine baffled them – the Second Coming. They found it hard to pray "Even so, come Lord Jesus". In their experience, that had been a get-out for facing life and coping with it exactly as it is. Jesus would come and put everything right – so you need not be bothered about sufferings now, either of others or of yourself. How could those who hungered and thirsted for justice be content to sit passively under conditions as they existed and just wait for the return of Jesus Christ? In their Bible study periods, the factory workers came back again and again to the theme. But that doctrine seemed alien. It did not come alive, as the others did.

Then came a terrible industrial accident. Six workers, including a Christian, were killed. There was a mass funeral of 1000 people. Both the pastor and the chairman of the Communist trade union concerned were given the opportunity to speak.

The pastor spoke for half an hour. His speech was divisive. He spoke of heaven and hell, the narrow and the wide gates. Those who were of his kind and view would be saved, others would be lost.

The Chairman of the Communist trade union spoke for only three or four minutes, but with great effectiveness. He pledged his union to fight for better legislation and better safety regulations; and ended with the communist exhortation to the relatives to go on living courageously.

The Christian workers were furious. Here was a time to express solidarity in the human family and Christians had been divided off from unbelievers. An opportunity had been passed up of witnessing to Christ's justice and judgement and healing.

Some of the new Christians met afterwards to give vent to their anger at the distortion of the gospel in the mouth of the pastor. One, in high indignation, blurted out "I wish Jesus had been there to speak for himself."

At once, for many, the key turned in the lock of the doctrine of the Second Coming. The Christian group began to see how poorly they represented Christ on earth – not only the pastor, but all of them. "Even so come, Lord Jesus" now meant something like "Lord Jesus, show your face and speak for yourself, for we are making an awful hash of representing you on earth!"

For that group now, the awareness of inadequate witness in the workplace and in the home, and the longing for truth to be displayed and make its own impact are gathered into the affirmation "He shall come again" and the prayer "Even so come, Lord Jesus".

A Theological Community At Work.

What does a theological community look like as it gets down to work? In his book *Love In Practice* (Search Press Limited) Ernesto Cardenal gives the following description of one theological community at work, detailing the different contributions which, in critical and supportive relationship with one another, enabled a company of fishermen, peasants, housewives, young people to get to biblical truth which was relevant in the Nicaraguan situation.

"Not all those who do come take an equal part in the commentaries. There are some who speak more often. Marcelino is a mystic. Olivia is more theological. Rebeca, Marcelino's wife, always stresses love. Laureano refers everything to the Revolution. Elvis always thinks of the perfect society of the future. Felipe, another young man, is very conscious of the proletarian struggle. Old Thomas Pena, his father, doesn't know how to read, but he talks with great wisdom. Alejandro, Olivia's son, is a young leader, and his commentaries are usually directed toward everyone, and especially toward other young people. Pancho is a conservative. Julio Mairena is a great defender of equality. His brother, Oscar, always talks about unity. The authors of this book are these people and all the others who talk frequently and say important things, and those who talk infrequently but also say something important, and with them William and Teresita and other companions that we have had and who have taken part in the dialogues.

I am wrong. The true author is the Spirit that has inspired these commentaries (the Solentiname campesinos know very well that it is the Spirit who makes them speak, and that it was the Spirit who inspired the Gospels). The Holy Spirit, who is the spirit of God instilled in the community, and whom Oscar would call the spirit of community unity, and Alejandro the spirit of service to others, and Elvis the spirit of the society of the future, and Felipe the spirit of equality and the community of wealth, and Laureano the spirit of revolution, and Rebeca the spirit of Love."

In the light of this movement, future resource centres, designed to equip people with a variety of forms of theological expertise which the total theological community will require, must be very different from present traditional Western theological colleges (except, possibly, where the needs of a small number of specialist scholars are to be taken into account).

It is becoming clear that professional theologians who live in protected situations must leave these and engage in the mainstream of life, if their theological work is to have relevance, quality and depth.

Change Is Possible

The Christian faith includes belief in metanoia – the possibility of deepgoing change in persons and communities, derived from the power of God. This enables people to act against their deepest inclinations and interests, in the name of truth.

At the heart of the Christian faith is forgiveness, through which the past can be dealt with genuinely and effectively, and fresh possibilities for life opened up.

It is a quite practical enterprise to set out to establish theology on a different base. The means to do so exist.

The manner of God's coming to us in the Incarnation is a sign of what is required to lay that base. The One to whom can be justly ascribed all wisdom and power was made known in human form; was born poor, weak and vulnerable. Jesus accepted life's terms exactly as others had to cope with them, without any special protection or favours. The essential theological statement God chose to make was made in flesh and blood, and in history. The conditions of ordinary life were accepted as offering proper means for communicating the deepest things of God.

Incarnation is separation overcome. It is dividing distance traversed. Keeping one's distance can be, literally, damnable. Immanuel, "God with us", is God's self-accreditation to speak not only to and for humanity, but from humanity. It gives an essential clue to us regarding how we are to live in our time.

How can theology be rescued and redeemed?

1)   A small number of specialists will, almost of necessity, need to devote themselves fulltime to scholarly work. The tension between pure scholarship and world-involvement will just have to be faced. Scholars are due a certain freedom to follow their twitching noses along interesting trails. Yet, left to their own devices, they may waste energies on false trails or follow leads which are of no consequence to the theological community. The theological community must assume responsibility to be critics and signposts for special-

ists – and still ensure that space is protected which scholarship requires to make its own demands and open out its own vistas.

Those thus abstracted from the ongoing life of the human community in order to undertake this technical work must, from time to time, be reinserted into the main flow of life (in rough and raw situations as much as possible, and without protection – that they might be put quickly in touch with realities which they do not normally encounter).

Here I must register one hesitation. The theological community includes within it many people who are educated and equipped to undertake work of scholarship. Might it be possible to distribute among them even the most technical textual tasks as well as the range of scholarly jobs at present being undertaken by theological specialists? Might the ground be more adequately covered than it can be by a much more limited number of fulltime professionals? The prospect is attractive and the project would be realisable. There are basic Christian communities which allocate to members the work of learning Hebrew and Greek, thus to provide a specialist scholarly resource at the heart of their enterprise. My own conviction is that a sprinkling of fulltime scholars throughout the theological community supplies a resource which nothing can replace.

2)   Other professional theologians will need to be trained in, and undertake their work in the thick of life. (If this locating of the work proves distracting, that must mean that, for theology, reality is a distraction.)

I can see your point but how do you expect me to THINK in that noisy world outside?

Our first and best theologian showed us the way. He was found in places and in company (company considered disreputable) where insights could be sharpened, judgements checked against life as it is lived daily, where the living language for knowledge and communication could be learned.

In the Partnership Between Black and White Project based at Selly Oak, theological educators from Birmingham University found that a non-traditional approach to Certificate of Theology work proved rewarding to lecturers and students alike. It involved training at weekends, when working people were free; sharing food as an integral part of the sharing of thoughts and discoveries; the tying together of study and acts of worship in black-led and white-led congregations; the drawing in of local people to share in the fellowship, training and discussion. It has become clear to those who took responsibility for this enterprise that the acceptance of unfamiliar situations, unfamiliar timing of teaching to take account of unfamiliar rhythms of life, unfamiliar partners in learning who have a different cultural background and history – can open doors to all engaged in the exercise to new understandings of reality. Theology, drawing upon richer resources of experience in the world church, becomes so very much richer itself. This is a church-related venture. How much richer still will be ventures which draw upon the wide resources of humanity for theological perception.

When professional theologians in their normal intercourse rub shoulders with shop stewards and managers, Pakistanis and West Indians, Hindus and Moslems, housewives and politicians, local action groups, the unemployed; when they are regularly found in situations of creative conflict instead of in withdrawn and protected situations: they will help theology to be, as it was meant to be, central to life.

The theological community itself has to work out disciplines for its growth and maturing. Within it, specialists in study and specialists in many forms of living need to learn how to build one another up for their service to the world God loves. The capacity to reflect deeply has to be trained and nurtured. Maturity needs to be won not only from the experience of doing and suffering but from fostering skills for mutual criticism which clarify, for any particular community, God's calling at a particular point of history. Latent gifts will need to be released and skills for interrelating them learned. It has been a fault of the church that church fellowship (greeting our brethren only) has been thought of as an end in itself − it will be an enrichment of the quality of that fellowship if communities are continually learning how they may both show love, and see that it is directed towards the accomplishing of Kingdom goals.

Much of the recent theology in the world church has developed from a fresh awareness of the mysterious place the poor hold in the purpose of God. Adopting the vantage point of their experience has been a mark of Liberation theology, Black theology, Asian Action theology and many theologies which might be called more subsidiary, such as Exodus theology. It must be acknowledged, in the same breath, that a good deal of sloganising goes on concerning theology which finds its springs in the sufferings of the poor. That angle of vision can provide interesting perspectives to thinkers who have no intention of moving from their secure seats, into contact with those they write about ! In different ways the poor get romanticised and tidied into systems of thinking which remain abstract.

I offer a test of the seriousness of new theological initiatives in Europe. Will theologically trained people be found alongside the damaged and disadvantaged and marginalised in society so that they can claim "I sat where they sat"? If this could be secured, there would be a great impulse to the reinventing of theology on a continent which is marked by theological traditionalism. God's terms for fresh vision often are: "Move from where you are to a place I'll show to you".

When the poor are kept at a distance and the image of God in them is defaced, there exists a standing testimony to the fact that the world is under the wrath of God. When the poor are lifted high, there exists a standing testimony to a world put right side up. Theology and testimony go hand in hand.

THE THEOLOGICAL SPECIALIST:
Redifinition of role

The attempt to tackle theology in an individual way, out of any vivid contact with the theological community; in protected situations, remote from the pressures and conflicts in which members of that community have to live; book-dependant rather than life-dependant for insights — has turned out to be a comprehensive act of robbery. It has robbed the world of that perception-for-engagement-where-it-matters, which should be the gift of theology to the whole of humanity. It has robbed the institutional church of concern about and resources for Kingdom conflicts and allowed attention to centre on ecclesiastical interests. At the same time it has made the theological specialist a "Protected Marginal", unchallenged in her/his field of work but with little impact on life.

The world, the institutional church, the theological specialist all need to look to the theological community to restore what has been lost.

It is not enemies but friends of the theological specialist who want to see the professional's monopoly of theology broken. Theology has a larger service to fulfil.

The Educated Cripple

"You really need to hear the peasants and farmers telling in their own way the theological perceptions they are coming to. I cannot go as deep or speak as clearly as they can. You see, I am an educated cripple — I had seminary training".

The speaker was Fr. Ed de la Torre. I was interviewing him when he was on the run from the police, before his first imprisonment. He was making the very serious point that training such as he and I received equipped us for certain theological tasks and, by the very fact that we were drawn into a special environment and into the company of the like-minded in a protected situation, disabled us for tackling whole ranges of theological work. However, where a theological community exists, i.e. Christians struggling for light in very diverse situations, this can be remedied. We can instruct one another, and build one another up. More often than not, the person formally trained will be mainly at the receiving end of instruction when the theological community gets to work. But there will be an important contribution to make too.

A. Limitations Of The Theological Specialist

1) The theological specialist has no **special** access to knowledge of God.

a) Theological training surely means minds brought to bear upon the knowledge of God and his revelation of himself so that his work and his nature are more clearly set out? That adds up to special access, surely?

The specialist has a contribution, as an obedient person and a person with particular skills – but, as a specialist, has no favoured access to knowledge of God. Jesus spoke of babes and sucklings getting the message of who he was. In his first letter to the Corinthian Church, St. Paul speaks of wisdom and cleverness offering no significant road to God. Knowledge of God is of such a kind that illiterates may be better instructed in the faith than professors of theology and have deeper perceptions about the meaning of the gospel.

Knowledge of God comes when God and human beings take one another into such serious account that they enter in to a deep, committing relationship. Knowledge derives not from mental activity but from life knit with life. The words for the sexual intercourse of Adam and Eve at the beginning of the Bible are the same as those for a relationship between human beings and God. The key to God's being and purpose is a shared life, in which he and human beings deeply enter into one another and search one another out. Once there is this committed relationship, the understanding which flows from that can be given acute and accurate interpretation by the trained mind. But people with little education may be able to articulate God's revelation of himself at least as well. An African woman, badgered by her neighbour because she was continually resorting to the Bible, was challenged, one day, thus: "There are so many books in the world ! Why is it that book that you keep going back to?" At last the woman was stung to answer. "Other books I read" she said, "that book reads me". Few Commissions on the authority of the Bible have got as far.

Moreover, God is made known not by the convincing force of intellectual argument but by the way life is lived. Note verses 15 and 16 of Jeremiah 22:

> "Think of your father: he ate and drank
> Dealt justly and fairly; all went well with him.
> He dispensed justice to the lowly and poor;
> Did not this show he knew me? says the Lord."

It is doing the will (something open to everyone) which communicates this knowledge truly.

b) As for the Word of God, God's self-communication – once again academics do not have a head-start over others. The Word of God is quite unlike words which can be most easily mastered by quick, trained minds. The condition on which persons and communities may hear the Word of God is that they make their life available. Then God's Word enters into the person or persons to "abide in" them. When God communicates, the terms offered to world-renowned scholar and teachable street-sweeper are the same; a readiness to allow him to fill that life and make himself known through that life.

The "renewal of the mind" alluded to in Romans 12.2 has no special tie-up with skills developed through education, mental capacity, intellectual prowess. In Hebrew/Christian tradition, the personality is not divided into bits which have different capacities for apprehending reality. Human beings and communities are whole persons and whole communities, with every part in organic relationship with every other part. It is not one aspect of the personality but the whole of the personality which is involved in the renewal of the mind. It is openness of the personality to God's renewing power, not brain-power, which can produce transforming change. And that is so for distinguished and lowly alike.

Knowledge of God, ability to hear and respond to his Word, the renewal of the mind — these are open to the theological specialist. But they are equally open to the whole community of faith.

The theological community has no place for know-all experts. It has ample space for gifted contributors. When scholar and illiterate open themselves to God and to one another within the community of faith, there will be no monopoly of theological perception which one can claim of right over against the other. There will be differences of contribution. There will be the building up of one another.

2) The theological specialist has no **separate** access to knowledge of God.

Generally study and expertise are thought to go together. Those who study are credited with possessing expertise beyond that which is open to others. Others can quite properly be expected to go to them and sit at their feet.

But when the study activity concentrates on God and his world, it involves a great variety of gifts and approaches directed to the attempt to penetrate the mystery of life. I tried to express this in an article for *The Ecumenical Review, Vol.27, No.3, July 1975, p.242*:

Study is a crucial resource for coping with life. It is far too important to be left to professionals and experts. God faces us with possibilities and intransigences in creation, in human society, in ourselves; with the need to take counsel with one another if we are to get the measure of these; with the call to act; with the certainty of reaping according to what we sow. All human mastery starts with humility before the terms set. Study involves us in the discipline of giving serious weight to such terms; taking the fabric of life, events, pressures, power-sinews, human resilience into account; doing justice to the character of the natural and animal kingdoms, the shapes of human personality, the forms of social structure, the lineaments of national and international institutions; drawing on the past; gleaning insights from the ends of the earth. This is done in order that, in relation to the natural creation (e.g. concerns for environment) human society (e.g. industrial and international relationships) and personal being (e.g. awareness of human make-up), human beings may be able to choose good ground and to sow well. Study implies a concentration of human capacities to gain critical discernment of those things which can enrich or disfigure life. It should help people to make mature human responses to the basic questions life poses.

The research undertaken by specialists is part of a large work of disciplined contemplation incumbent on human beings in face of the marvel of God and of his creation. Again, it is a contribution made alongside others – e.g. that of the couple who take up the cudgels at persistent evidence of lack of equal opportunities in a male-dominated society and do the necessary homework to counter it; that of shop stewards who are driven, by evidence of dehumanising processes of work, to ask more fundamental questions about the purposes of industry. No one form of carefully-researched accesss to reality can, of right, claim precedence over other forms.

B.   Lack Of Theological Skills

The theological cripple needs to look to others who have the theological skills he/she lacks.

1)   This means giving up the idea that, because you are theologically trained, you can make judgements in fields outside your experience. The Bishops of the Roman Catholic church, celibate

males, debated marriage and family life in their 1980 Synod, using lay people as consultants. It does not seem to have occurred to them that it was the lay people who were experts, who were in a position to do the theology. The bishops might have usefully acted as consultants to them. The Church's real theological resources are continually wasted in this way.

As a preliminary to our conference on Sex and Marriage we shall have a short role-play. Father McGinty —you can be mother....

2) The specialist is tempted to think of theology as a deposit, rather than something which is constantly being won and lost in a struggle for light. To undertake the main work of theology demands a situation from which the specialist is most often remote – a praxis situation in which there is interplay between developments in history and the struggle to determine the mind and purpose of God. Gospel perceptions were worked out in conflict situations in the early church – Peter and John being helped to get their theology clear by being hauled before a Jewish court and forbidden to speak and teach in the name of Jesus; Peter being made to struggle with the opening of the young Christian church to Gentiles in full partnership, spurred by the visit of a Roman enquirer, a vivid dream, and a situation of tension regarding certain aspects of the Jewish tradition. Events challenged existing understandings of the faith. The faith challenged events.

The remoteness of many specialists from the conflicts of our day – the outcome of which will thrust life in one direction or another – is a theologically disabling factor. Even that illumination which the specialist could provide for the church by supplying knowledge of past conflicts and their resolution – which could throw light on present conflicts — may be denied by scholars who are so separated from the mainstream of life that past conflicts are presented all ironed out and unoffending.

Mainstream theology must be done where the pressure is on, and in very mixed company.

3) I see little evidence that theological specialists, when they are trained in their art and craft in colleges, are given skills to recognise and interpret the theological underside of events. The ability to analyse and interpret developments in political, social and industrial life; to take the measure of policies being worked out by different parties; to seek to establish the essential value-systems which underlie these policies; to develop a theological critique of implicit views of life and propose theological alternatives from which different policies might be developed — appears to be almost entirely wanting. The result is that, in a situation of riots, strikes and picket lines, the theological specialist is liable to react in a class-determined way, and develop some theological rationalisation for that reaction: and to have nothing significant to say at that point to other members of the theological community. When it is the specialist who is turned to, the business executive is left in her or his wilderness, deprived of that critical support which Christian faith should provide.

In these areas, the professional theologian is almost always found to be a broken reed, deficient in theological skills (apart from those related to matters concerning family, neighbourhood and, possibly, educational institutions).

IF I didn't happen to Know that you have had no theological training I would have said that your last remark was something of very great importance

4) Language, which should light up the meaning of life, forms a barrier. Those of us who are theologians so often use an in-language of an abstract kind from which the juices of daily life and conversation have been squeezed out. This abstract language can form a code which the people of God cannot crack. It can withdraw the basic questions regarding the faith from those who have to live the faith: and confer a kind of secret society status upon an elite. The dessicated language theology employs at the professional level is a handicap to theology as an illumination of life. Jesus used Aramaic, the language of the people, rather than Hebrew, the language of religious professionals.

But Albert if God had wanted you to talk about things like that he would have given you letters after your name!

5) It may seem that, whatever theological skills are trained out of those who undertake a theological education and a scholarly task, one province remains exclusively that of the scholar — the systematisation of theological beliefs so that their relationship to one another and their role in giving a coherent explanation of life under God, are put at the service of all who search for meaning in life.

But   The organising centre of the Christian faith is not a constellation of beliefs, but a redemptive act which brings into being a community which is called to live the truth.

The truth is a person, not an intellectual construct.

In the history of the church, the organiser of lived truth is the Holy Spirit.

A coherent declaration of the truth as it affects people at any point of history must find expression not in formulae or 'the deposit of faith', but the lived faith of the church in different parts of the world. It will not be a set of constructs but a breathtaking shimmer of light.

A special contribution of the scholar is to put this lived faith in telling relationship with faith as it has been expressed in different ages and stages of the development of the church's life. The professional theologian has a special service to render in putting what is lived and affirmed today into the context of the Communion of Saints, all through history, and to the ends of the earth.

Christians who seek to do justice to the range and consistency of Christian belief must open themselves, in a hearing of faith, to every other part of the world church, and to the instructive action of God outside the church, and share, criticise and delight in the fullness of faith. This fullness will never be formulated by experts. It will always be open to discernment by the humble. Such discernment will lead more naturally to adoration than to formulation: for it means that the fullness of him who fills all in all will be recognised as in-dwelling the church on earth!

C. Lack Of Stringency

The theological specialist takes pride in a rigorous, scientific approach to the evidences presented to the church. Within the terms of an academic discipline, there can be justified satisfaction in the careful and diligent work of scholarship, for academic terms may provide the only dependable, checked means for getting at certain aspects of the truth. More will be said about this. Meantime, attention needs to be paid to great areas where there is a lack of stringency in the work of the theological specialist.

The theological specialist is, often unawares, captive to a Western tradition which has for too long been taken to be universally applicable. Educational assumptions, modes of thinking, ways of ordering research, mental stockades are rarely brought under sharp scrutiny to have their validity established or discounted. They put their stamp on all finished work. This imprisonment within a culture often exists unrecognised and unacknowledged. One result can be that material and methods from outside Western traditions may be treated as exotic; or as offering raw materials for processing in Western theological factories; or as providing a new flavouring for the Western academic broth − without real change taking place. It has taken the rise of Third World theologies to challenge the status of traditions of theology which have dominated for so long, and to bring into question what has been for so long unquestioned.

Quite inadequate allowance has been made for the influences of professional interests and conformities, personal ambitions, human hang-ups — all of which put in jeopardy the objectivity of work done.

Theology has also been seriously class-bound. From other parts of the world the insights of farmers and industrial workers, women, men and children, have produced challenge to traditional theological interpretations of life; whereas, in Europe, there has been a kind of tunnel vision of God's work in the whole world, the walls of which have a class character. Where are our working-class theologies? Where are there Bible studies which come from other than people with much the same educational background and class-definition?

There are other elements in the tunnel vision. Unrecognised sexism wreaks havoc on interpretations of life's meaning and the priorities for faith which can only be worked out in true part-nership. Racism is often undiagnosed. But class-blindness is par-ticularly damaging.

Thank God a theological community exists, spread all over the world, rich with diversity of experience, brimming over with the gifts of the Spirit. At least we in the West who are theologically so far behind others have a world church to which to go for instruc-tion, if we are prepared to be humble and teachable.

* Skills for living and suffering must be directly related to skills of scholarship: expertise in such things as sustaining life through daily work and rearing families must be kept in vivid interplay with expertise which assesses the character and judges the validity of biblical texts and other evidences.

* Complementary skills for taking account of reality must be drawn upon: academic study skills must be accompanied by those for measuring, analysing, contemplating, absorbing many forms of reality, of "feeling the life" through all the body's antennae, of discerning the way the human race is moving.

* Different forms of logic and perception must be taken into account, so that spoken cultures, sung testimony, silent con-fession, danced affirmation are given their due, alongside the written word. Theology today is not so much found in verbal formulae as in letters from prison, testimonies before tribunals, communal decisions in face of government pres-

36

sure, poems, reflections on industrial futures, cloth tapes-
tries (those in Chile which contrast Pinochet's reality with
God's), musicals like *Jesus Christ, Superstar.*

* Everything that is done theologically will need to be re-
vived and renewed again and again through the discipline of
discipleship, embracing repentance, forgiveness and sancti-
fication, which brings us level with ourselves and provides
remedy and healing for our sin.

* In particular, theology and spirituality must not be separated.

We are fortunate to live in a period of history when the theological community is giving evidence of a new quality of spirituality.
Features of it are a deep and vivid relationship with Jesus Christ,
acute awareness about how people are placed in the world, con-
stancy in prayer and in sacramental nourishment, political
engagement, loving care for others, a common life in which there
is both sharing of goods and truth-telling. To those who have had
the privilege of living with basic Christian communities in different parts of the world, it is clear that their life is all of a piece and
that what determines its development is the power of the Holy
Spirit.

In many ways the Solentiname Community provides a significant illustration. The different gifts of the people are drawn upon
and the scholar-theologian accompanies the people, often raising
sharp questions but without demanding that she/he be given the
last word. What the specialist lacks can be supplied by the theological community and what the community lacks can be supplied
by the specialist. In this way, the scholar is much more central to
the life of faith than has been the case traditionally.

Always mainstream theology must be done by the whole theological community, in and for the human community.

The Specialist's Restored Role And Place

The experience of Paco is instructive. I lived with him in a
barrio in Nicaragua. Previously he had been my contact for the
Participation in Change programme of the World Council of
Churches, when he was based in Paraguay. He had seen the
growth of basic Christian communities and acknowledged how

disturbing this was for himself and his fellow-priests in Nicaragua: "We were scared" he said, "we were really scared. We saw these communities developing, encouraged them all we could, felt that they were of the Spirit. Then we discovered that there was hardly anything committed to us as priests which they were not able to undertake in their ministry. We were teachers of the faith? Giving and receiving from one another around the scriptures, they were much more effective teachers of the faith. We were leaders of worship? Building into the liturgy their own music and drawing into it their own experience and suffering, they were much more skilled at worship-making than us. We at least had the Mass? But it became clearer and clearer that we were not in control of the Mass, that it was an act of the people together, whatever place of prominence we might take. And when it came to living out the faith in the world — of course they had a maturity and an awareness of what was at stake which went quite beyond anything that we were heir to. We were really scared! We thought that if we gave them their head, there would be no ministry left for us. We would be redundant.

"But we felt that it was commanded by the Spirit that the rich ministry of the people be allowed to develop. So we did not stand in the way. The result? What we lost is given back to us with new power and depth. The people understand the place of the ordained priesthood as never before, whereas we have a ministry which is no longer over them, but with them. It was when we were prepared to give up the ministry as it was that God gave it back to us as a new thing".

Professional theologians who are prepared to give up their isolationist positions to help the developing theological maturity of the church, may hope to get a new role — much more communitarian, much more relevant to the life of the world, much more eagerly sought after by members of the church, much more limited in scope and much more effective in impact.

Real fears will need to be worked through, as well as those which ultimately stem from defensiveness.

Can the work of doing theology be open to all and sundry? Does it not need special skills which cannot be picked up in the street; and application which entails withdrawal from the mainstream of life? Have we not had experience of populist theology producing a misshapen faith?

1) In the total theological task, careful and exacting scholarship

will always need to be given a high place of importance. The continuing work on the state of the original texts; the differences between these, and attempts to discover how variants came about; the use of texts in different contexts; currency given to fresh interpretations, and fresh discoveries which throw new light on old positions; new questions or theories arising from fresh angles of approach – of course this work of scholarship provides an essential element in the activity of the theological community. Imagine Ernesto Cardenal at work, in a community of landworkers, fishermen, men, women and children on an island of Lake Nicaragua. They work on a biblical passage, share what it means to them, absorb or challenge one another's interpretations. The scholar allows all this to go some way. He may then point out quietly that the original manuscript on which the text is based was in a poor condition. Have their interpretations been entirely dependant on that text? Are there other parts of the Bible which make much the same point? If it proved that a certain phrase was likely to have been a later insertion, or was found in few manuscripts – would they be forced to go back to scratch and start their search for light all over again? The scholar at the heart of the theological community has a contribution to make which questions and checks – but which does not give the theological specialist the final word of judgement: for the specialist is theologically crippled or even incapacitated who is not also challenged and instructed within the community.

But there are difficulties. Surely some will need to be given the job of doing scholarly work and nothing else? The skills of scholarship need to be developed over a lifetime rather than over a decade. In this age of world-wide communication, simply to keep in reasonable touch with what is happening in one's chosen field in different parts of the world, requires a total involvement. The sharpening of tools must go on, and every year lands an increasing amount of material on the scholar's work-bench: new discoveries are made, new theories advanced – they have to be investigated, evaluated, judged. Some break-through may require any scholar or a group of scholars to go right back to base. How could part-timers cope?

The other side of the picture is that the specialist may be occupied with mere theological embroidery, remote from life's reality if the theological community is not there to insist that what is central and pressing be given scholarly attention.

THEOLOGICAL EMBROIDERY?

Don't you agree its beautiful even though no-one can understand its meaning

Should the specialist be allowed to withdraw from the main part of life, provided that there is reinsertion in the mainstream at some tough points, at agreed intervals? Or can the theological community keep an eye on the work of full-time scholars so that they may remain full-time on the job, and yet be given no peace if they concentrate on the fringes of life rather than its heart and centre?

2) It will be part of the specialist's responsibility to challenge populist theology which may produce a mis-shapen faith.

The Christian community has certainly, in history, been no more guilty of distorting the Gospel than were scholar-theologians. But there are warnings from the populist cult of Mary, for instance, which argue that scholars have a discipline to bring to bear which can bring balance and health to what might otherwise go to excess and emotionalism.

Any real scholar will stay open to conviction that break-outs labelled as merely populist may at times be more accurately described as the church rediscovering its faith and taking responsibility for its life!

40

There are times when the commitment of scholars to the truth, whatever may be the religious fashions of the day, and their readiness to swim against popular tides will be of signal importance.

3) The scholar will not only need to be prepared to stand against people's power where that threatens to distort the faith, but against clergy power. For a great part of history, clergy have exercised control over the church and have found mandates in scripture and tradition to justify this control. The job of the scholar will not be to produce "supporting evidence", but to produce evidence – whether it supports or runs counter to existing ecclesiastical positions. A test of the integrity of scholars of today will be found wherever the official church has to be confronted in the name of truth and they are summoned to answer before tribunals!

TOOLS AND TECHNIQUES FOR THE REINVENTION OF THEOLOGY

Theological specialists who are prepared to go into new territory can find fresh and different scope for their gifts. They can play their part in shaping tools and techniques for the reappropriation of theology as the people's work. It is on the cards in our time, in a measure unexampled in history, that lay people, or rather the church as a whole, laity and clergy together, may, by main force if need be, take into their own hands the theological task which is properly theirs. It is incumbent on those of us who are theological educators to encourage this to happen.

Why say "by main force, if need be"?

41

To be deprived of one's theological responsibilities is a serious disinheritance. It is to be deprived of some part of one's share and lot in God's kingdom (which we may take briefly to be 'life structured God's way'). Exclusion from what God wants people to have is too serious to be taken lying down.

A strange saying in both St. Matthew's and St. Luke's gospels gives the use of force a natural place wherever attempts are made to exclude people from the Kingdom. The Kingdom is to be taken by storm. Violence is assumed to be a necessary ingredient of persisting faith.

With the coming of John Baptist and the heralding of Jesus Christ, an old state of affairs came to an end. The one who was greater than John opened the kingdom of heaven to all believers. But there were obstacles in the way – tradition, habit, those who occupied positions of power and prestige now threatened. The way to the new inheritance was barred.

What must those who had been invited to claim this new inheritance do? They must not allow themselves to be excluded. They must take, by main force if need be, what God means them to have.

Powers, religious and secular, are to be confronted if they deny place to those to whom God has given place.

But the Kingdom is spoken of in two ways. It is not only to be taken. It is given by God. Those who have power to obstruct the movement of people to claim their inheritance in Christ may, by grace, choose to be rather something like partners with God in his giving. That will mean encouraging the theological community to accept theological responsibilities. It will mean a search to find positive ways of restoring to the theological community their proper task. it will mean discovering and inventing tools and techniques for that restoration.

As theological specialists, we can give people confidence in facing up to their theological tasks. Fr. Ed de la Torre, in the Philippines, finding the mystique ascribed to the priesthood an albatross around his neck, argued with the people in this way:

"You say I am the one who knows, because I have been ordained a priest: right? Then listen to the one who knows. As the one who knows I tell you that you, together, can perceive what God is like and what God is doing more clearly than I can, and you have a ministry to fulfil which is more

42

significant and complete than mine, in which mine plays only a part. Take that from the one who knows!"

So he persuaded them, as the one whose authority they acknowledged, to recognise their own authority and task and ministry.

It will not be easy, in the Continent of Europe, to persuade people – who for so long have been made strangers to their theological responsibilities, and have been encouraged to believe that they did not have the wherewithal to undertake them – to bend to the task. It may take a long time for the mental shift to take place which allows them to accept as genuine their theological calling. It may take a long time for them to accept the full discipline of being the theological community. They may often look back with envy at the old, simpler, situation where they could say: "Leave all that to the theological specialists!" Quietly, persistently, patiently, those who have taken as their remit what belongs properly to God's community must give the community confidence for tackling the work. God's people must gain a new respect for their own gifts, for the foundation for understanding God's work in the world which comes from their own experience, for their own language as the fittest for theological thinking and articulation, for their capacity, drawing upon one another's resources, to analyse situations and relate them effectively to insights gained from Scripture.

But to give people a new confidence is not enough: we are all pretty lost about how power and responsibility may be transferred from the few to the many. Means need to be found to develop theology in different constituencies and by different methods. The basic Christian communities in Europe speak about the re-appropriation of those things which belong to the ministry of the church which have been taken over by specialists, and particularly by clergy. We need to fashion tools for the re-appropriation of theology, and develop techniques which help it to be reinvented as the people's work. The theological specialist, seizing a fresh opportunity and adopting a new role, can make a contribution to the growth and maturing of the Church at this point of history such as has rarely been open to him or her.

We are at the very beginning of fashioning tools and techniques of this kind – at any rate in Europe. What I can share concretely comes from my experience in the Department of Mission, Selly Oak Colleges, which has probably two gifts in particular to offer to

Britain and to the rest of Europe −

a) insights from the world church which allow it to recognise clues for tackling our task in our own part of the world, and

b) doing theology in relation to living situations.

In the development of tools and techniques of the kind mentioned, it is people's work which must fill the picture, the theologically trained person being simply one of the contributors who − sometimes by articulating some things more clearly, by showing links where none had been recognised, by pressing questions − throws back upon the theological community responsibility for and illustrates the possibility of tackling their work at a deeper level of critical seriousness. As has been said, people's own experience must be honoured. The thinking and speaking must be in language which is their normal form of communication − to relapse into a specialist, more abstract form of language will be to take responsibility away from them. Without being uncritical about their assessments of situations and the relating to them of scriptural perceptions, these must be seriously noted and given their intrinsic value − not valued from some abstract and distant measurement of acceptability. The rhythm of involvement and reflection which is natural in their way of life must be adopted − however awkward that might be for those who want meetings and events to be accommodated to their diaries (who can control their use of time, as most people cannot). The theological specialist will be with people, sit where they sit, as much as possible; will fit in with their timing; and will adjust to their way of doing things.

Accordingly, there will need to be different approaches and contact with different constituencies.

A. Approaches

One can adopt methods for day conferences of about sixty people and week-long conferences of over two hundred, which will encourage people to see and value what is already important in their experience, and recognise how it can be built on, thought about critically, and given more effective expression.

When day conferences are set up and someone is asked to introduce each session, all that is left to the whole body of people is to react, positively or negatively, to what has been presented to them. The more brilliant the speaker is, the less are they free to think their own thoughts and make their own contribution.

The alternative is to replace speakers with resource persons; and plan preparation to find out what, in their situation, participants are facing or should be facing. Agreed homework is then done in anticipation.

To be concrete – in an area of unemployment, the homework undertaken was to study four passages from the Bible relating to work and its significance in life and then visit –

a)   a family in which the breadwinner had become unemployed

b)   a situation where two salaries had been coming into a household and now there was only one,

c)   young unemployed people, whether they had ever had a job or not.

The question to struggle with was how the understanding of life in scripture related to the actualities of life; especially to what work had meant when people had it, what it was seen to mean when they lost it, and thus what significance it held.

Once the conference takes place, it is those who have done this homework who are the catalysts. They share and check theological insights, working in small groups and then in plenary; identify pastoral responsibilities; commit themselves to forms of action; and, using their own words, draw into worship the longings, discoveries and rejoicings which had surfaced over that day of encounter. The specialist gives the people confidence that the work is properly theirs; helps the process to develop so that they may make the most of what is theirs and of what is given by others; and is ready to intervene to add some theological reflections, or question some findings.

This basic form was adopted by a Conference of the World Alliance of Reformed Churches European Council, held in Romania in September, 1980. In preparation, those who came from most countries in Europe were asked to think more acutely, over a period of months, about the way they were and should be living the faith in their own particular situation. Over 200 assembled.

On the morning of each day, representatives met in relatively small groups speaking French, German or English, shared their insights, tried to see which were the commanding concerns of the

45

majority of the group. At a later point in the day, a representative from each group shared these with a co-ordinator. The three co-ordinators, with a chairman, spread out the material, put their finger on what they thought were the commanding concerns emerging from groups, and developed a dramatic dialogue for presentation in the evening, so that issues which were important for the Conference on any particular day were played back to the assembled delegates and their visitors. This helped participants to get some idea of where the whole Conference was moving, without infringing the integrity and the right of particular groups to develop their own agenda. The next morning, groups could either say "Interesting that so many groups are on to this or that question – we must put it in our own agenda" or "What we are following through has its own importance, whatever else the rest of the Conference is fastening on. We'll stick to it". There was no need for a key-note speaker. Everything started with what the members of the Conference themselves saw to be important. Yet their contribution was given perspective and challenge by the contribution of others; and it was woven together with that of others.

B.   Constituencies

The Christian Action in the World Conference, initiated by the Department of Mission in league with a number of other church bodies and agencies, deliberately set itself to reach beyond the usual church conference constituencies. For this purpose, it drafted letters to employers and trade unions, to make a case for getting working people off work for a few days without loss of pay. Once people met, they were asked to take reponsibility for the dynamic development of the Conference, although a rough plan had been made out beforehand which they could scrap or alter at will. There was no follow-up. Follow-up plans emanating from the quarter from which the Conference had been initiated would have meant assimilating participants to organisational ways and thought-patterns on the basis of which the Conference had been developed. It would have meant a domestication of those who took part.

Much did come out of that Conference, of its own right and in its own way. Those who organised it were asked to confer at a later point to see how they might provide resources for developments in three different parts of England. But it was a frail attempt to get beyond the usual middle-class constituencies, and it only partially succeeded in doing so. The reaction of a gardener, approached over six months before the Conference took place, was instructive: "The description of the Conference is gobbledygook. The way it is set up is not the way I would do things. And who knows what he or she will be doing six months ahead?" Clearly we had hardly begun to take into account the different rhythms, ways of life, ways of communicating which lie outside our middle-class orbit – which mean that most people outside that magic circle may be disabled as far as efffective participation is concerned, from the start.

Others, however, gained new confidence in themselves as the theological community, as the following quotations testify:

"The people want their God back. They want Him unwrapped from a cottonwool theology of ancient words and times and put back in the market place. They are not content with theology for theologians. They are eager to relate their faith to life and call on the ministry for 20th century parables, dynamic Bible study techniques and a new lead in 'doing theology'.

"People at the conference showed they did not want to be protected from theology by the church accounts and the building extension, the bazaar and the flower festival. They want to think about their God. They want a vigorous and sinewy theology for industrial and political man and are prepared to share responsibility for developing it in a language that is clear and relevant."

(Jean Silvan Evans)

"The method of Bible study was so engaging that it gave people (and I talked to some of the lay people about this) a new sense of the aliveness of scripture and its resourcefulness to daily life.

"Most of the lay people wrestled with the question of compromise – or toleration. This questioning was done around structures in their work place and was very concrete to them. For some of the lay people I spoke to, they felt freed by having others to talk with about this and to be reminded that Christianity isn't about black and white answers most often.

"There was a lot of strength on the part of the lay people when they became clear about how they want the clergy to help them – they want theological input and help to look at the Bible, but they don't want lectures. They want help in meeting with other Christians who struggle with responding to the structures in the work place — want to be able to think Biblically with other people and have the minister as resource. This is a great statement to hear from lay people."

(Margaret Marquardt)

The Conference "A Theology for Britain in the '80s" was not in any way specially related to the Department of Mission. But it was an expression of the same kind of concern as marked the "Christian Action in the World" Conference. It took that concern further, more effectively. Only a small number of theological educators were invited. The main body consisted of some who had been marginalised by society and yet who had not given way to bitterness but developed constructive criticism from their anger and frustration; those who worked alongside them in society: and some Third World theologians. The aim was to get a new starting point for doing theology in Britain (an associated enterprise had the same aim for Western Europe) developing theology not from abstractions but from the suffering, deprivation, resilience and joys of those who know the rough edge of our society. An Irish twin-conference was much more successful in fulfilling that aim.

TOOL MAKING

1. Narrative Theology

How is the biblical text to be brought alive so that it becomes gospel for people today? How can the work of the scholar be put at the service of the total Christian community? These are questions which Walter Hollenweger and John Davies have struggled with, to the profit of those who have had the chance of working with them. They have forged new tools for the tasks to be tackled.

A world movement to make theology central to life is still in an early developing stage. Third World theologians such as Juan Luis Segundo and James Cone have located exegetical scholarship within the universal community of Christians. (The menace that this represents to secular powers-that-be is witnessed by the harassment that Dr. Segundo has had to suffer. It is clear that theology can become a dangerous threat.) In parts of the programmes of the German Kirchentag and in the work of Dr. Hans-

Ruedi Weber we find illustrations of a search in Europe to partici-
pate in the movement to place academic theology at the service of
the whole people of God — but the movement is still little understood and appreciated in academic circles in Europe.

Walter Hollenweger plays a significant part in the search for
alternative ways of doing theology. He is Professor of Mission at
Birmingham University, and offers one lecture and one seminar
period per week in Selly Oak Colleges as part of the agreement
when the chair was established. In these periods he develops, with
mature students, work such as he has been propagating in a
number of contexts and countries, on Narrative Theology.

Two basic affirmations underlie his work:

a) The scholar has a decisive part to play in making the gospel
come alive in our time: she or he has skills and resources to which
lay people do not have access. The expertise of the scholar needs to
be affirmed as strongly as ever, and given a central place.

b) The people of God have many forms of expertise in living to
which the professional theologian does not have access except
indirectly through them. Dr. Hollenweger writes:

> "In the final analysis, it is the people of God (which also
> includes the theologians) who are responsible for theology.
> Today, however, those members of the people of God who can
> think theologically and want to enter into that critical pro-
> cess which in my opinion is necessary for the understanding
> of the Bible, are denied their theological responsibility sim-
> ply because their culture does not include the tools of critical
> exegesis."

So what is looked for is a meeting of different kinds of expertise
in which knowledge gained from life-perceptions and knowledge
gained by the use of tools of critical exegesis play complementary
parts. This allows different ways of apprehending reality to contribute to a rich texture of relevant theology.

The establishing of a creative partnership between the scholar
and the people of God releases worlds of understanding and languages of life into interplay which would otherwise have lain dor-
mant. These worlds and languages are there in the biblical texts.
They are needed for the interpretation of these texts so that they
come alive. Scholars who have access only to the world of scholarly assumptions (produced by people with much the same educational background, who adopt a roughly similar way of evaluating

and organising material) and whose language is the jargon of theological scholarship, cannot do justice to them. A larger frame of reference is needed. The narrative theology approach supplies it.

A larger frame of reference than that of traditional academic scholarship is equally needed if theology is to make sense to all kinds of people and is to be built up from different worlds of understanding and different languages of life. These, as things are at present, professional scholarship has habitually set aside and disinherited. Their contribution is needed if the gospel is to be heard in our own time in its fullness and richness. Take the languages, the perceptions of reality of those who have been economically and culturally disinherited. Theologically, these have been refused value and place. They have been adjudged unscientific, unusable for the purpose of making precise scholarly statements. In narrative theology they are given new place – and reveal an accuracy and adequacy for certain apprehensions of reality which other languages cannot match. At the same time, they are not given a final place. Other languages are not, in their turn, devalued and set aside in favour of the "language of the poor", as if it alone had validity. It is rather held that, as the scholar abandons theological responsibility if she or he adopts uncritically the language of the powerful, theological responsibility is likewise abandoned if the theologian becomes merely the mouthpiece for the aspirations and ambitions of the oppressed.

Something more creative than such alternative stereotypes is in view. Dr. Hollenweger has described the interest which guides him in narrative exegesis in the following way: "I understand the church to be the place where theological and economic class-struggles and conflicts (and the two belong together; this we gladly learn from the Marxists) are organised in such a way that new creative interests and practices emerge from it."

* * * * *

It is difficult to describe, in the abstract, ways of doing theology which rely very much on both scholarship and imagination. It is particularly difficult to explain narrative theology without illustration. I have been given permission to use material from an article by Dr. Hollenweger on Intercultural Theology published in October 1978 in the magazine *Theological Renewal*. The excerpts given in that magazine are extracted from a longer narrative exegesis.

Three stages in such work are distinguishable:

a. The Scholarly Foundation

A great deal of time and exegetical skills need to be invested in laying such a foundation as only careful scholarship can supply. The text must be worked on thoroughly, commentators consulted, and then, as Dr. Hollenweger has said: "I have to walk around, you know, and talk to the people imaginatively who are involved, until I find a framework." This exact and exacting work provides evidence which is taken into account and a story is developed which incorporates that evidence. It is now very clear that the story does not provide some general illustration of the text and speculation upon it, but contains within it the essential exegetical substance which brings the text alive.

This laying of a foundation for the narrative on the church in Corinth is described in the following way.

If one reads the first epistle to the Corinthians purely as a document of religious or theological struggle, then one misses its dynamic contribution to intercultural theology. On the other hand, if one reads it as a document of a complex struggle, if one considers the sociological profile of the church of Corinth, then one sees the biblical text not only as a theological rationalisation of an underlying cultural struggle, but also as a scenario for creatively organising our cultural, social, political and religious struggles within Christianity today.

What is the sociological profile of the church in Corinth? If we analyse carefully the list of the names and the professions of the members of the Corinthian church we can distinguish three social groups with clear cultural, social and religious characteristics. The first group consists of rather wealthy and influential freemen. They were property owners such as Titius, Justus and Gaius. The text makes it clear that the Christians gathered in the houses owned by these men for their meetings. These villas must therefore have been reasonably large. Krispus, formerly chairman of the synagogue also belonged to the group. A chairman of a synagogue had to have considerable private means as he was partly responsible for the up-keep of the synagogue. The most interesting person in this small but influential group was Erastus,'ho oikonomos tes poleos'It is not quite clear what this title means. It must have something to do with civil engineering, real estate and the general management of public works in

51

Corinth. It is certainly the case that Erastus was an influential member of the Corinthian society, and this would be further endorsed if the inscription found in Corinth in which an Erastus is documented as a director of public works in Corinth can be attributed to the Erastus mentioned in 1 Corinthians.

The second group was the largest. It consisted of uneducated slaves and dock-workers, many of them foreigners. Their leader seems to have been a woman, because the term 'hoi tes Chloes' cannot refer to a family but can only mean 'the people of Chloe' or perhaps 'Chloe's clique'. It is well-known that the Christian slaves complained that they were not properly treated and did not have enough to eat at the meetings because they could only get there late at night after they had finished work whilst the better-off arrived earlier and over-indulged both in food and drink.

Finally there was a third group. Tertius might have belonged to this group. They were the educated slaves, secretary-slaves, house-slaves and scribes who worked for the Roman administration, the banks and the port authorities. They were perhaps what we would call today something like the middle-class.

There were at least three identifiable areas of conflict between these three groups. There was the conflict between Erastus and Chloe's people (i.e. between the first and the second groups). After all Erastus represented the ruling colonial administration when he became a Christian.

The slaves did not expect to be freed in the secular society, but they did expect – and Paul backs up their expectation – to be of equal standing in the church. This in itself was revolutionary, or perhaps even 'spiritually subversive', because the pagan religions were generally organised along the cultural and social divides – just as most Christian churches are today.

The second area of conflict was that between men and women. As women became prominent in the Christian church, there emerged marked tension between the place of women in society at large and the place of women in the church.

The third area of conflict is the most important for our purpose. It is the conflict between social groups one and three on the one hand, and group two on the other hand, that is, the conflict between the educated Christians and the illiterate or semi-literate slaves. Many of the educated Christians had been introduced to the great texts of the Septuagint. They were certainly able to read the Greek Old Testament and the letters of Paul. The uneducated slaves (group two) probably did not even speak Greek properly. It is quite understandable that these slaves relied much more on their spontaneous inspirations, on speaking in tongues, on visions and prophetic insights which they could identify with the risen Christ, whilst the educated Christians emphasised intelligibility (i.e. what they understood by this) and the historical connection of their faith to Judaism and the Hebrew Christians in Jerusalem.

It is in this cultural context that Paul introduces the theological model of the body of Christ. This is – at least in Paul – not a mystical body but a social body with an identifiable sociological profile. Paul's theological model is, however, 'sociologically dysfunctional' and politically suspect. The body of Christ is a social entity which by its very existence is a challenge to pagan social and cultural stratification, to pagan apartheid – to pagan snobbery on the one side and to the inverted snobbery of 'dockworker exclusivism' on the other side, even and in particular in its theological and ideological disguise.

The narrator of the following story, *Conflict in Corinth*, is a secretary-slave in the Corinthian Bank of Trade and Commerce. He is invited by his friend Tertius to several meetings of the Christians. He observes these Christians and reflects on their interpretation of a piece of propositional theology by their founder Paul (1Cor. 14). In other words, it is an attempt to broaden the hermeneutical discipline by integrating exegesis into the cultural, political and social context in which theology had and always has to operate.

b. The Story

The exegetical work undertaken in preparation seeks to answer not only the question asked in Western theology "What did the author want to say?" but a question too rarely asked "Who were the recipients of the story and in what context was it received?" The narrative is designed to offer a language and a platform to people who are not biblical specialists, who do not know the jargon of biblical scholarship, yet can enter into a meaningful and informed dialogue to discover what it was like when people originally concerned heard a word which became Scripture.

The story *Conflict In Corinth* develops as follows:

I arrived late at Gaius's house the following Sunday. Because of the riots in the port and the risk that some of the ships might be set on fire, we had to complete some urgent insurance transactions. I could not leave the bank at the usual time and arrived at about half-past seven.

Women should not speak in public

When I entered his villa I heard strange singing. It seemed as if the whole citizens' meeting of the Christians was singing in ten or twenty parts. I could not understand the words. I soon realised that this must be the singing in tongues which I had heard mentioned several times in Paul's writings. Although everyone sang his own melody so to speak, the harmonies fitted together. It was as if the Christians were building a temple of sounds, a social-acoustic sanctuary under whose roof they could feel at home.

Unlike my first visit I was not able to sit with my friend Tertius. He told me that it was customary for new comers, the non-initiated, to be seated in special places, on benches at the back and down the sides. These benches were called 'Idiots'-Seats' because those sitting on them were considered by the Christians to be uninformed, uninitiated, idiotai. Sitting on one of these seats I was able to observe the service very well.

The distribution of wine and bread followed the pattern of the previous Sundays. I do not need to repeat this. However, when Erastus, the chairman of the department of public works in Corinth, went forward with the scroll from which he intended to read and when two torch-bearers took their positions at either side of him, Chloe rose to her feet and protested.

'With respect, brothers and sisters', she said, 'how can you just carry on with the reading from the learned texts of our brother Paul after all that has happened in our city during this week? Do you not know that Jason, whom we baptised last Sunday in the name of Jesus, and who has been baptised with us together into one body, as Paul says, that this same Jason is in prison? Does Paul not say that if one organ or limb suffers, all suffer? And Jason suffers. Do we suffer with him? Do you know that he has been unjustly accused of rioting? It is surely clear to the gentlemen and brothers from the city administration here present' — and she looked at Gaius and Erastus, but glanced also briefly at Tertius – 'that if the accusation can be upheld in court, his crucifixion is inevitable. Two weeks ago Tertius read from Paul's letter, "God has put the various parts of the body together, giving special honour to the humbler parts, so that there might be no split in the body and that the parts might care for each other". Jason is in serious trouble. Why do we not care for him?'

Some of the slaves and dock-workers who had gathered as usual on the left-hand side of the inner court of the villa around Red Chloe, stood up. Erastus held up his hand as if he wanted to say something, but Gaius began to speak and said somewhat brusquely to Chloe, 'Sister Chloe, Paul does not favour women talking publicly in the citizens' meeting of the Christians'.

'That is your invention, brother Gaius', she protested. 'No' Erastus replied, 'Here it is written: Women should not address the meeting. They have no licence to speak, but should keep their places as the law directs. If there is something they want to know, they can ask their own husbands at home. It is a shocking thing that a woman should address the congregation'.

Chloe was silent for a moment. Then she took courage and said, 'You would like that Gaius, wouldn't you? You want to re-introduce the Jewish law. But this law was abolished by Christ. And what husband should I ask at home?' Some laughed, as they knew she was not married. 'Anyhow', she continued, 'may I see the passage?' Chloe went up to the table and was shown the scroll. 'That is in another handwriting', she commented, 'and furthermore these sentences are written on a different piece of parchment which has been stuck on later. I do not believe that this was written by Paul. This is contradicted by other things he writes. Have we women not received the Holy Spirit just as you men?'

The slaves, both men and women on the left-hand side of the meeting, broke out in a wild tumult. 'Praise the Lord. Yes, amen'. Only Phoebe from Cenchreae remained silent. 'And', Chloe continued, 'has Paul not said that women should wear a veil when prophesying? That is why I bought this red veil.' Then she concluded in a soft voice, 'I would prefer to remain silent if one of you gentlemen would take up the cause of the accused slaves. Do you not remember what happened last year? Amongst those crucified who were exposed in a long row of crosses at the port, there was a Christian. The leaders of the riot had heaped all reponsibility on him and tried to capitalise on the general suspicion and contempt for the Christians.'

Living with conflict

Chloe sat down. Gaius had listened with great attention. 'Chloe is right' he said. 'We must send a delegation to the pro-consul, and it seems to me that you, Erastus, should lead that delegation. We have to inform the pro-consul that we consider that to convict Christians of rioting is politically unwise and unjust and that we would not hesitate to appeal to Rome against the ruling of the courts in Corinth in order to stop what we consider this miscarriage of justice. True, "love endures all things, believes all things, hopes all things", but that does not mean that we accept without comment a criminal breach of justice. Paul also says that "love does not enjoy injustice but rejoices with truth" '.

I thought to myself: But suppose Christians were accused of undermining society because the very form of their worship-service questions existing law and order? Would it not be a just accusation, because in their services foreigners, slaves and women are considered equal – or almost equal? This could be seen as a kind of spiritual revolution. Their belief in a coming kingdom of God which will be inaugerated by the last trumpet, surely relativises and questions the existing Roman Empire. Nobody in his right mind can question these facts. It is possible that Jason is justly accused according to Roman law. And if he is crucified according to the law, what will Erastus, Gaius and Chloe do then? I could not answer my question.

In the meantime the excitement had died down. Red Chloe and her people seemed to agree to Gaius's proposal. The torch-bearers approached Erastus and he began to read again. 'If I pray in tongues, my spirit prays but my mind remains sterile. What then? I will sing with the spirit, and I will sing with the mind. To sing with the spirit', Erastus looked up from the manuscript and added, 'refers to that which we did at the beginning of our meeting when all sang together in tongues in many harmonies. To sing with the mind refers to that which we did last Sunday, when we sang the hymn which we all know "And yet abideth . . ." According to Paul both have their place in the service. I continue – If you sing with the Spirit how shall the one who is sitting on the seat of the idiot, the uninitiated' – and all looked over to me – 'how shall he understand what you

56

pray? You may go through a wonderful religious experience, but it is of no help to the other man.'

'We do not sing and pray for the others' Quartus, one of the two slaves who had been baptised the previous Sunday, took the floor. He had been taken into custody on a charge of alleged rioting and he had been scourged, but then released with a warning to mend his ways. 'We sing and pray for us', he said. 'There are certain things which we have to do for our own benefit as almost everything that we do is for others. For instance, being punished and scourged for others.' His hand touched his back and his face looked half comical, half sad. 'Always carrying bags for the rich people, always working for others. At least in the worship service we would like to do something for ourselves. There we sing for us, and speak in tongues for us.'

'Amen, amen', shouted the slaves on the left-hand side of the gathering.

Erastus continued, 'Paul is not against speaking in tongues. The next sentence shows this very clearly. He writes: "Thank God, I speak more in tongues than all of you, but in the congregation I would rather speak five intelligible words for the benefit of others as well as myself, than thousands of words in tongues. Do not be childish, my friends. Be as innocent of evil as babes, but at least be grown-up in your thinking.'

'Paul is unjust and he does not understand us', Quartus interrupted again.

'Certainly, we should be grown-up in our thinking, but we do not think as the scribes, like Erastus, Gaius, Tertius and Paul think. We are Christians without books. You think with a pen in your hand. You think in sentences and arguments. We think in images and visions. We think with the whole body not just with the head. Do you really think that my back does not think when the whip is dancing on it, or when I carry heavy bags on the docks? Because we think with the whole of our bodies, speaking in tongues helps us to grow up in thinking. Why can't you ever understand this? We can't afford the luxury of limiting thinking to reading and writing. It is bad enough that for ten weeks already we have had to listen to Paul's letter.'

'Do you want to hear the rest of the letter?' Erastus asked.

'Sure we want to hear it' Quartus replied. 'We want to know

what Paul has to say. But we shall always protest when we disagree'.

'That is right', Erastus said, 'that is part of the body, part of thinking in the body, as you say, that conflicts are not suppressed. However, Paul is concerned not only with Christians but with the world as a whole. He thinks that our service must make a newcomer so understand his own innermost being that he will fall on his face, worship God and recognise that God is in fact in our midst.'

I found this argument a little strange. I had never felt like falling on my face and declaring that God was in their midst. This did not bother me but I still found it strange that they believed that their crucified Jesus was both in their midst and that he would come again. To my way of understanding, these were two very obvious contradictions. On the other hand I was not disturbed by the singing in tongues and the emotional outbreaks from Chloe. On the contrary, the human, sometimes almost primitive spontaneity of the Christian worship, their direct way of dealing with each other, impressed me.

I do not know why, but all at once there was complete silence in the villa. Almost everyone sat with his eyes closed. They prayed in silence. Erastus stood at the table with the scroll in his hands, flanked by the two torch-bearers, I could not say whether this silence lasted for moments or for half an hour. Suddenly I felt something rising in me. At first I though that I was going to vomit. But it was something else. I feared that I was going to weep in the middle of this awful silence. I did not know why. In desperation I grasped a corner of my tunic and put it in my mouth. I do not really know what happened to me. It is of course true that I do not have a proper identity. I do not know where I belong. The old Greek religion has been so changed by the occupation of the Romans that it is almost unrecognisable. It does not speak to me. The oriental mystery religions are too Saturnalian for my taste and the synagogues of the Jews too strict. I cannot feel one with the uneducated slaves, and the more educated people in Corinth (even if they would accept me) are too superficial. If I could have it my way I would like to be a free-floating religionless sceptic. Then my status as a secretary-slave would not bother me. Can one live like that? As an antagonist – especially if one is committed to a bank?

The Christians again sang their hymn 'And now abideth . . .

.' 'and now abideth faith', some sang, while others continued, 'And now abideth hope.' A third group added, 'And now abideth love.' Then all three groups joined together to sing, 'But the greatest of these is love'.

Too good to be true, I thought.

Erastus continued his reading, but it no longer interested me. He read, 'Of the prophets, two or three may speak, while the rest exercise their judgement upon what is said.' Erastus stopped. 'The others shall exercise their judgement', Tertius repeated, 'that means, for instance when Chloe is prophesying, that we, the others, who have also received the Holy Spirit, evaluate her prophecy. It means that when Paul writes a letter to us we exercise our judgement on whether or not we can recognise God's will in his writings. The others are those who confirm the inspiration of a prophet, a teacher, a writer – or reject it'.

Erastus continued from Paul's letter, 'If someone else, sitting in his place, receives a revelation, let the first speaker stop.' 'Amen, amen', the slaves shouted. Erastus went on, 'You can all prophesy, one at a time, so that the whole congregation may receive instruction and encouragement. Prophetic outbreaks are subject to the control of the prophet, for the God who inspires them is not a God of disorder but of peace.'

A strange ending, I thought. Paul did not write, 'God is not a God of disorder but of order'. He did not go so far as to identify himself with the apostles of 'Law and Order', with the port authorities and against the rioting slaves. He did not speak of 'order' but of 'peace'. On our way home I asked Tertius how he understood the final sentence. 'Order', Tertius said, 'can only be understood hierarchically and statically, as a power which rules over others. That is not what Paul means. For Paul "peace" means to name and suffer conflicts – sometimes even to live a long time with them – without destroying the community in the body of the Lord. Peace means that we recognise Chloe to be an organ in this body, even if she makes us suffer sometimes. And obviously we make her suffer too.'

'And what do you think about that alleged insertion concerning the place of women in the meeting of the Christians?' I asked him this apropos Chloe. He replied, 'I wrote a letter for Paul once about three years ago. It was addressed to the Christians in Rome. I wrote it without charging any fee for Paul's and Christ's sake. During and after dictation he got me to alter the wording quite a lot. Sometimes he told me to cross out whole passages and replace them. So it is not impossible that he also wrote this passage. But I must say that the style does not sound at all like his and the statements certainly are in contradiction to other things he has written. But then Paul is not a very logical writer. On the whole I would agree with Chloe. It seems unlikely to me that Paul wrote this passage himself. Somebody, possibly a well-meaning secretarius, has put it in. Perhaps the letter has been read already to another house church in Corinth and maybe they have added this section. We are going to write to Paul and ask him for further clarification.'

Shall I become a Christian?

We said good-bye and I returned alone through the night streets of Corinth. I live in a small room in a villa belonging to one of the directors of the bank where I am employed. There I keep the few things which belong to me – a second tunic, sandals, parchment, a bed and a lamp. Every day I go to the office in the bank where I work as a secretary-slave. I am responsible for cheque transactions, general book-keeping and I have to make sure that letters of credit and coins are always correctly filed and put away, especially in the evening when the bank is closed. In uncertain times, as had been the case this week, I have to work overtime. Once or twice a year on the great public holidays we close the bank for a whole day. The Corinthians drink so much that it is advisable to close and see that the bank is securely locked up.

I am a slave and my master is a director of the Corinthian Bank of Trade and Commerce. He treats me well. I have enough to eat and a small room. When I need anything I can go to him. Only I do not know where I belong. I belong neither to the free business men, the officers, the scientists, the bankers, nor do I belong to the slaves and dock-workers who, so they say, think not merely with the head but with the whole body. Perhaps, if I am lucky, I will be given my freedom one day. It happens, but it depends on the goodwill of one's master.

So I ask myself whether or not the citizens' meeting of the Christians is the right place for me. I cannot be a whole human being all on my own. I need Chloe's people and also Erastus and Gaius and my friend Tertius. But, being a Christian has great disadvantages. Christians run the risk of being regarded as non-conformist or even hostile to the state. That is because so many of the Christians are slaves. Numerically they are in the majority, but they do not have as much influence as the minority of the free and affluent Christians. Membership in the body of Christians means a tremendous increase in prestige for the slaves. But, as I have already said, to be a Christian has disadvantages. One could easily be identified with Chloe's people, and if one is arrested and convicted of conspiracy it does not really matter whether one is guilty or not. A just conviction or a miscarriage of justice produces the same result. One is dead.

What shall I do?

Is there any good reason for becoming a Christian?

Do I need any reason for becoming a Christian?

c. The People's Part

The work of scholarly exegesis, presented imaginatively in narrative form, is now tested within the body of believers: for "The exegesis of the future is an exegesis to which all the charisms contribute, all 'the interests', all the cultures, female and male insights, all the gifts in the Body of Christ," Dr. Hollenweger believes. The biblical text has come alive. It sets up resonances with contemporary questions faced by many kinds of people in many kinds of situations.

Those who have been part of the community accompanying the scholar may say "Now I would like to tell you that story within the context of the Carrs Lane Church in Birmingham — in terms of a debate going on there (or within the context of my church in Southern Italy, or New York, or whatever)." When people develop work of this kind, they are recognisably the specialists. They are the experts, because they know the ingredients of the situations they have to work with. They know directly the factors which have to be taken into account. They are encouraged to release their imagination to grapple with situations they face as Christians in their own time. The biblical story illuminates that way.

Take another example. Imagine that there are, in one community, Christians involved in multinationals on the management side and others engaged in building up trade union combine committees to be a check on the multinational's power. They are prepared to engage in a serious search for insights from the Bible to help them deal with particular responsibilities (as managers, shop stewards, consumers). The scholar-theologian, realising the need, might draw their attention to the story of Zacchaeus, and undertake work to uncover the situation in which that story made impact. The scholar would not pay attention to the question usually asked "Why did Jesus call Zacchaeus?", because to this question the text does not give an answer. The text arose in the church of Luke, in a context where you had rich people as members of the church. They were involved in marine trades – many of them, especially women, becoming rich, having their own businesses. They found themselves troubled by some parts of the Christian tradition – sayings like "Blessed are the poor". A debate was going on in the church: what about the rich? So Luke told them the story of Zacchaeus, which is particular to himself and does not appear in the other gospels. It makes it clear that rich people get into the Kingdom of God under two conditions. The first is that they share their riches with other people. The second is that what they have gained unjustly (whatever that means in the context, which is highly debatable) they have to give back. It is under these two conditions that rich people can enter the Kingdom of God.

Once Christian communities today can talk not simply about Jesus and Zacchaeus in face-to-face encounter, but about the church of Luke and the context which gives point to a specific story or parable of the gospel, the imagination of all kinds of ordinary people can be brought into play. This allows them to transplant the story from the original context into their own contemporary context so that it illuminates the very questions which disturb them, questions related, for instance, to the power of multinationals and the rise of combine committees.

2. The Bible Workshop

John Davies, then Principal of the College of the Ascension, has developed practice and theory for encouraging all kinds of people to gain humble confidence in handling the Bible together and finding how it speaks to their life today. He was one of the staff team of the Department of Mission who has been most concerned to see how the work in Selly Oak may be put at the service of the churches, particularly those in the Midlands. Accordingly, what follows should not be thought of as something simply taking place in class-rooms, but something also developed in partnership with people in rural areas, inner cities, and dioceses. The occasion is a Bible Workshop, a regular part of the programme of the Department of Mission, offered both for students in training and church members who want to add to their insights and skills.

He describes the "Bible Workshop" approach as follows:

We are in the age of the second Christians.

The first Christians were the people immediately affected by Jesus and his friends. A mixed group they were. The first Christian, in the sense of the first person to acknowledge the gospel of the crucified Son of God, was a professional man of violence, a non-commissioned officer of a colonialist army of occupation, one of several centurian heroes in the New Testament. Another first Christian, in the sense of the first person to recognise the Risen Christ, was also a pretty unlikely character who had somewhat lowered Jesus' credibility among the respectable and had an alarming history of mental derangement: further, the fact that she was female would have made her testimony inadmissable in a contemporary court of law. On her evidence, and on the evidence of a collection of other unimportant and improbable people, millions of us have accepted Christian faith. These people remembered the activities of Jesus and kept on with his commitment to the Kingdom of God. They were the first Christians.

But soon another generation of Christians emerged. They also had to work out their commitment to the programme of the Kingdom which Jesus announced. But their situation was different. They were not living in Jerusalem or Galilee: their problems did not centre round the arguments of temple officials. They were living in Gentile areas, Antioch, Ephesus, Rome and Corinth: their problems centred round the relationship between Jew and Gentile, where Gentiles were the majority. New questions faced them, questions to which the stories of Jesus could give no direct answer because Jesus had not faced them. Jesus had never given an answer to the question, "should Jews and Gentiles eat together?" It was a question which had not arisen in his experience. So these "Second Christians" could not ask, "what did Jesus say?" But they could ask, "Is there anything in our memory of Jesus which can help us find our own answer?" And this was much more helpful. They could reflect on their own experience and link it with the experience of Jesus. They found in their memories of Jesus an

immense store of resources with which to face their unprece-
dented questions. And this was why the stories of Jesus were
treasured and recorded: they proved useful for enabling a disciple-community to do its work.

Samuel – you and your
friend can stop arguing about
Who can eat with Whom – I've given your
dinners to the children...

Now, we in our day are also "second Christians". We also face
new questions – questions which cannot be answered simply
by turning up the appropriate page in a book of instructions.
People are not vacuum cleaners or carburettors automatically
transmitting power and putting it to use. Despite all the mar-
riage-manuals and baby-care books, there are some things
which people have to learn themselves for the first time. Being
a Christian community is something like that. We are the early
church for our time. No-one has ever been here before us. No-
one has ever been us before. But we can learn from the example
of these comrades in Christian discipleship of 1900 years ago.
We can reflect on our experience, link it with the stories of
Jesus, and derive mandates for the new action in our contemporary world.

We read the New Testament for this purpose, and for this
purpose only. The New Testament is not aimed at giving us
more information. It does not aim to give us facts about days
gone by, or to give us an uplifting spiritual experience, or to
supply texts for propagandists of social improvement. The New
Testament is a resource for a community committed to the
programme of Christ's kingdom, which faces problems and gets
into trouble precisely because it is thus committed. The New
Testament is all about transformation, the transformation of

individual persons and of the universe. It is about Christ's programme of remaking creation so that it becomes true to the mind and purpose of the Creator. To treat it as merely an object of historical or literary study, or as a source of individual solace, is to misuse it, to bend it from its purpose: it is like using a chisel as a screwdriver — it is bound to make a mess.

We are the Body of Christ. From the New Testament we see what the Body of Christ gets up to. The Body of Christ makes gospel events in the days of Jesus of Nazareth and in our day. We move off the line of our ordinary routine, our contemporary history, and pick up the Gospels: we look back to the events of Jesus: and then move back into the line of our contemporary history to make new gospel events in our present world.

But when we look at a page of the Gospels, we do not see only an event in the life of Jesus: we see an event in the experience of the "second Christians" too. We see something happening in the churches of Mark and Luke. We see the effect of Jesus on the life of a later community; we see what appealed and made sense to the Christians of the second generation. And the original activity of Jesus is, as it were, an event within an event.

In applying the method, perhaps two emphases need to be identified:-

1. At an early point in the engaging with the passage of scripture, people are encouraged to get into it themselves by relating to some element within it in terms of their own experience or attitudes or feelings. It is necessary at an early point that people should feel that they are genuinely part of the story in some way or another, and not merely "students" of the story. This is to enable them to feel and know that the Bible is their book, and that in the Bible they are in contact with the Lord who is their Lord and not just somebody else's a long way away.

2. Early in the study, it is necessary to make the clarification of purpose, namely that we are going to the Gospel material to gain resources so as to enable us to be more effective as agents of the Kingdom of Christ to which the Gospel material testifies. We are not interested in this material simply as "students"; we are "trainees" or perhaps "artisans", seeking resources for a job which is laid upon us. This is not merely a matter of getting our own intentions correct; it is also a matter of getting into focus with the original

author. We need to identify with Mark or Luke or whoever as our brother and colleague, writing to enable the church to face its contemporary problems in the light of the stories concerning Jesus. In this pattern, we are doing exactly the same thing as the Christians in about AD 70 were doing, who were seeking to answer contemporary questions for which there were no precedents in the Gospels, but who believed that by searching their corporate memory concerning Jesus, they could gain resources for facing these contemporary problems.

A full scale Bible study of this kind can be worked out illustratively at Selly Oak so that people see the point and grasp the method; but its true place of belonging is not in some educational institution, but quite specifically in the context of a group of people who have got a commitment to continue working together. In the conventional church this would be a synod, or a presbytery, or a parochial church council, or a congregational consultation, or something like that. Equally, it could be a house group, a basic Christian community, a group whose commitment is in the work place or some other place of engagement in the world. The Bible-study programme **ought** to yield mandates which can be applied specifically within a local programme.

A BIBLE STUDY METHOD

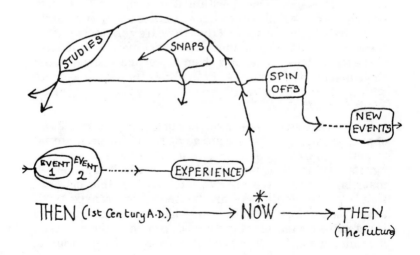

THEN EVENT 1 is a story in the gospel-narrative.

EVENT 2 is the witness and active life of the first Christian community, which remembered and used the story and wrote it down.

NOW Now we are at the point marked *. We take time off from our ordinary programme of life: we pick up the Bible: we read a passage which describes an EVENT in the activity of Jesus.

SNAPS – connections with our immediate experience.

What does the story connect with **in your experience?** What bells does it ring in your memory?

What little details in the story interest you? Why?

Are there problems for you in the story? Is it offensive to you in any way?

What character can you identify with? What does it feel like to be that character?

Would you like to be the teller of the story? Why?

STUDIES – the EVENT in its original context, read more thoroughly.

Do you see anything interesting about the place which the story has in the Gospel?

Why do you think the evangelist was interested in the story?

Why do you think that our fellow-Christians in the early church were interested in the story?

SPIN-OFFS – we turn back into our present situation.

What message or mandate do you get from the story,
    for yourself as a disciple of Christ,
    for yourself as part of the suffering world,
    for your disciple group as the Body of Christ,
    for your neighbourhood,
    for the world?

Who or what is being commended by the story, in contemporary terms?

Who or what is being criticised?

What new attitudes are encouraged?

67

↓ What **new action** is suggested for the disciple-community today?

THEN * We go back to our ordinary programme of life.

↓ We are the Body of Christ; Christ will create new Gospel-events through us.

3. Social, Industrial and Political Issues

Ian Fraser's starting point for developing theological work in relation to living situations is attentiveness to the terms of the contemporary situation itself. The process used must take care:

— never to transpose the burning concerns of people struggling for light and justice in the world into some alien sphere of thought,

— never to rob such people of their own language in favour of an in-language which does not communicate with them where they are,

— always to take seriously the complexity of situations, the many factors at work in them,

— never to give to some expert or experts the only word that matters, particularly the last word.

1. Appropriation of the situation

It is important for the whole group to "own" its work. Only thus can all the members hold responsibility for it. The following means are employed to ensure that this is so.

When e.g. Social Responsibility Officers meet with a resource person or animator to choose a tough, complex living case study to work on:

* The resource person does not know which situation-study, of those suggested in outline by members of the group, will be chosen. So there is no means of manipulating the process from above.

* Once the group has selected a situation-study, it is presented in more detail. The person who has given the study is then asked to stay silent while the group reconstruct it,

68

listing the main factors in its development. They challenge and correct one another. Only when the group is satisfied with its version, is the provider of the study allowed to make a final check on its accuracy. Now the situation belongs not only to the provider but to the group.

* At any point in the process, members of the group can demand a change in the pattern of development. A basic method, worked out beforehand, is there to start with. But not in even one instance has that method been followed through exactly as you would find it on paper. Alert groups keep seeing the need for some extra element of analysis, some adjustment of the steps proposed for disciplined group thinking. What is preserved in every case is the rigour, the thorough work to expose the essential features of the situation. Situations themselves are unique and demand their own particular adjustment of agreed methods.

By these devices the group makes the work its own. Only when it owns both the subject for its thinking and the process by which that thinking is developed, will the work come alive for participants. Only when it owns the subject and the process, will the common theological task be recognised and tackled by the group.

It then becomes important that the group's "knowing", as that has been established by their work in common, becomes the basis for what follows.

The provider of the situation-study may now be asked to supply more detail. Once supplementary questions are answered, a guillotine comes down. No further probing into the background of the situation is allowed, because

- the request for more information at all kinds of odd times can be a diversion from the job which must now be tackled

- in real life, people have to deal with situations in the terms of data which, however carefully checked, will be bound to be incomplete.

The main features of the development of the situation, now teased out, are listed on the board and checked. As far as the group finds possible

- the pressures falling on human beings are pinpointed,

- human consequences are evaluated and registered,

—   the major powers at work are identified.

Once all this is recorded on the board, a careful search is undertaken for one or two "handles" – some cluster of factors which might allow the situation to be grasped so that something may be done about it.

This part of the work is best done by getting people to consult two-by-two. They then make their own contribution, submit it for criticism and criticise the contributions of others – until there is a group agreement on substantive findings. This method is also employed at later stages to provide for thorough cross-checking.

2. Values – Probe

Regarding the slice of life which has now been pretty thoroughly spread before the group, the next task is to

a)   identify the policies being pursued by the principal parties in the situation

b)   assess the views of life and value judgements underlying the policies themselves (**not** the explanation of the policies offered by their respective promoters)

c)   develop a theological critique of these views and values.

At this point, if so desired, there can be a significant use of theological experts who have until then remained outside the process. The group itself has, till now, been absorbing, in a detailed way, the elements of a particular situation. The exposure of these main elements has allowed it to undertake relevant theological work. In the bygoing, however, the group may also unearth some more general questions deserving attention. Take an example.

A group has chosen a complicated problem based in an inner city in Britain in the '80s. It has taken account of the pressures and powers which influence the evolution of that one particular complex of issues. But a nagging question persists in the mind. It concerns not one particular city at one particular time in history, but the development of cities as such. Is the building of cities in the purpose of God? Is that activity rather, Babel-wise, a challenge to God's authority? What does the Bible say, what variety of views or single view does it express?

A panel comprising an Old Testament scholar, a New

Testament scholar, and a scholar from some part of the world church outside Europe has at times been assembled, to share biblical and world perspectives. The panellists are not given information about the way the group's work has developed: the value of their contribution lies in the objectivity of their reactions and reflections. When, as most often happens (although there is a hit-or-miss element) this contribution meets the members of the group right where they are, there is tremendous impact and illumination. Said one participant in the summer of 1981: "I came away with some tremendous insights and some real learning. The contribution of the panel on Thursday was stunning, and I am still wrestling with 'law and grace' and 'reality' and 'the unmanageable'!"

3. Making Decisions on a Faith Basis

From this point there is a search for

- an alternative theological basis for dealing with the situation
- a delineation of policies which might be developed on this basis
- the testing of such policies for realism, particularly by persons who will be involved in implementing them.

The group has now developed a strong sense of community. Members have not only gained insights for facing their own tasks. They also know some problem-areas intimately and the attempts of colleagues to cope with them. they may now well add the offer of personal back-up. "If it would help that one or more of us join you for a day or two days, should things come to a head, shout us in", they will say before parting.

1. APPROPRIATION OF SITUATION   The Apostolic Element

Development Of Situation	Pressures Falling On People Involved	Human Consequences	Major Shaping Powers At Work	"Handles" Or Entry Points
Identification of crucial points in the unfolding of the present challenge to action.	Tension effects, not only on those primarily affected but families, neighbours etc.	What people have to cope with, e.g in terms of changed status, security, opportunity; community attitudes.	Listing these (e.g. Government agencies, Employer's Federations, Trade Unions) may also disclose less visible forces which manipulate significantly.	Can this group put its finger on one or two crucial areas where something can be done, previously listed factors being taken into the reckoning?

2. VALUES – PROBE

The Prophetic Element

Main Policies Promoted Or Advocated	Values Underlying	Relevant Biblical Resources	Theological Critique
These can often be reduced to 2 or at least 3. Listings must be fair to supporters of each policy proposed.	At an interim stage, a question mark can be put against disputed underlying values. But overall group judgement must be decisive eventually.	Particularly at this point, a process of listing all references; submitting them to challenge; defence by protagonists to produce an agreed reference base is important.	The company should now be able to make an assessment of policies on the basis of their search for relevant faith insights.

3. TAKING DECISIONS   The Obedient Witness Element

The Theological Ground	Policies Consonant With This Ground	Action Required	Check For Realism	Sharing Of Intentions; And Solidarity Covenants
At times this ground is already implicit in the theological critique. But if there is distrust of policies already advocated, the laying of a theological ground-work may have to be tackled from scratch.	One or more existing policies may gain the conviction of members; or some new and different policy may need to be sketched out.	This may be worked out in the total group; or groups formed according to each line of action advocated. Possible alliances with those outside the church can be assessed.	Particularly if a fresh line is advocated, there must be hard debate on whether proposals are practicable or merely idealistic vapourising.	Members of the group share what they are going back to do. They may also covenant with one another "Call us in, if the going gets tough where you are".

CURRENT PUBLICATIONS OF THE IONA COMMUNITY

PEACE AND ADVENTURE   ISBN 0 9501351 6 X
     Ellen Murray

THROUGH WOOD AND NAILS   Record No.146/REC/S
     Iona Abbey

THE WHOLE EARTH SHALL CRY GLORY   Paperback   ISBN 0 947988 00 9
THE WHOLE EARTH SHALL CRY GLORY   Hardback   ISBN 0 947988 04 1
     Iona prayers by Rev. George F. MacLeod

WILD GOOSE PRINTS No.1   ISBN 0 947988 06 8
     John Bell & Graham Maule

WHAT IS THE IONA COMMUNITY?   ISBN 0 947988 07 6
     Iona Community

A TOUCHING PLACE   Cassette No.IC/WGP/004
     Wild Goose Worship Group

A TOUCHING PLACE   ISBN 0 947988 09 2
     John Bell & Graham Maule

WILD GOOSE PRINTS No.2   ISBN 0 947988 10 6
     John Bell & Graham Maule

COLUMBA   ISBN 0 947988 11 4
     Mitchell Bunting

FOLLY AND LOVE   Cassette No.IC/WGP/005
FOLLY AND LOVE   ISBN 0 947988 15 7
     Iona Abbey

90 RECIPES FROM THE IONA COMMUNITY   ISBN 0 947988 17 3
     Sue Pattison

GRACE AND DYSENTERY   ISBN 0 947988 19 X
     Ron Ferguson

EH...JESUS...YES, PETER...?   ISBN 0 947988 20 3
     John Bell & Graham Maule

FREEDOM IS COMING   Cassette No.IC/WGP/006
FREEDOM IS COMING   ISBN 91 86788 15 7
     Utryck

CLOTH FOR THE CRADLE   Cassette No.IC/WGP/007
     Wild Goose Worship Group

CO-OPERATION VERSUS EXPLOITATION   ISBN 0 947988 22 X
     Walter Fyfe

WILD GOOSE SONGS – VOLUME 1   ISBN 0 947988 23 8
     John Bell & Graham Maule

WILD GOOSE PRINTS No.3   ISBN 0 947988 24 6
     John Bell & Graham Maule

THE CORACLE – REBUILDING THE COMMON LIFE   ISBN 0 947988 25 4
     Jubilee reprint of Foundation Documents of the Iona Community

GOVAN OLD PARISH CHURCH   ISBN 0 947988 26 2
     John Harvey

WILD GOOSE SONGS – VOLUME 2   ISBN 0 947988 27 0
     John Bell & Graham Maule

THE IONA COMMUNITY WORSHIP BOOK   ISBN 0 947988 28 9
     Iona Community

RE-INVENTING THEOLOGY   ISBN 0 947988 29 7
     Ian M. Fraser

MEANING THE LORD'S PRAYER   ISBN 0 947988 30 0
     George T. H. Reid

EH...JESUS...YES, PETER...? BOOK 2   ISBN 0 947988 31 9
     John Bell & Graham Maule

Other publications are in preparation, please ask for details.